"All over this nation, God is stirring the hearts of men to rise up and enter into their God-given destiny. Lou Turner's lifelong passion is to see men enter into their divine purpose in life. 'Living Life God's Way,' of which this book is a part, is born out of this passion. Throughout this Bible study series, Turner opens up God's Word to help you discover HIS plan for your success in your life, family, and work. If you are ready to get off the treadmill, to begin to enjoy God's fullness in your life and make a significant contribution to the world around you, I recommend that you dive into this life-transforming Bible study."

Hal H. Sacks, D.Min., *BridgeBuilders International Leadership Network*

"It seems North American culture is rapidly moving toward what the Bible calls 'everyone doing what is right in his own mind' (Judges 21:25). The prophet Isaiah declared, 'Woe to those who call evil, good, and good, evil' (Isaiah 5:20). This Bible study series will challenge every man in the 21st century as 'iron sharpens iron'! The Q&As at the end of each chapter really personalize the teaching."

Dennis Conner, *Co-Founder/President, Called to Serve Prayer-Coaching Ministry*

"I have known Lou Turner for over twenty years. Lou loves Jesus and has built his life on the Word of God. Lou's Bible study series, 'Living Life God's Way,' is full of biblical truth that has been tested and can be applied by disciples of Jesus in practical ways. These books will help you grow in your faith and gain confidence and competence, which will increase your fruitfulness in Christ.

Mark Buckley, *Founding Pastor of Living Streams Church*

Living Life God's Way

Being a Leader

Lou Turner

Being a Leader
First Edition, 2020
Copyright © 2020 by Lou Turner

Being a Leader is part of the Living Life God's Way Men's Series by Lou Turner.

All rights reserved. No part of this publication may be reproduced, stored in a retrieval system, or transmitted in any form by any means—electronic, mechanical, photocopy, recording, or otherwise—except for brief quotations in critical reviews or articles, without the prior permission of the publisher, except as provided by U.S. copyright law.

Unless otherwise identified, Scripture quotations are from the ESV® Bible (The Holy Bible, English Standard Version®), copyright © 2001 by Crossway, a publishing ministry of Good News Publishers. Used by permission. All rights reserved.

Scriptures marked NKJV are taken from the New King James Version, copyright 1982 by Thomas Nelson. Used by permission. All rights reserved.

Some of the anecdotal illustrations in this book are true to life and are included with the permission of the persons involved. All other illustrations are composites of real situations, and any resemblance to people living or dead is coincidental.

ISBN: 978-1-7331186-7-5

To order additional books:
www.hislifeinus.com
www.amazon.com

Editorial and Book Packaging: Inspira Literary Solutions, Gig Harbor, WA
Cover Design: MTWdesign, Dickson, TN
Typsetting: PerfecType, Nashville, TN

Printed in the USA by Ingram Spark

He will be like a tree firmly planted by streams of water,
Which yields its fruit in its season
And its leaf does not wither;
And in whatever he does, he prospers.

Psalm 1:3

TABLE OF CONTENTS

Preface　ix

How to Use This Book　xi

Introduction to Being a Leader　xiii

1. Qualities of Godly Leadership?　1

2. What Is Leadership?　15

3. God's School of Leadership　29

4. Biblical Qualifications for Leadership　39

5. Leadership in Action　49

6. Start Where You Are　73

7. Being a Leader Is Not Always Easy　83

A Final Word　91

About the Author　93

PREFACE

We live in a world that has largely forgotten what manhood is about. In the Western world, men are often portrayed on television as buffoons who are out of touch and must rely on their wives to straighten them out. These characters are portrayed as silly, insensitive, lacking common sense, and when they do speak, they are usually wrong. They are often portrayed as either ridiculously weak or overly macho. They are not able to commit to a long-term relationship and generally mistreat women. Positive role models are hard to find in the media.

However, the Bible teaches a different type of manhood, the authentic one. Men are to be leaders, loving their wives and children, excelling in their work, and standing for truth. They are to be men of wisdom, knowledge, having godly character and seeking after God and His direction. They are to be exhibiting godly leadership at church, in the community, and in business, and to be a light to those around them. They are to be men of compassion and love, as well as courageous and bold when needed.

Men go astray from these ideals, including Christian men, due to improper convictions or beliefs about life. They have received these from various sources: well-meaning family and friends, the media, and the culture around them—a world system that promotes the tearing down of God's biblical truths.

But without proper biblical foundation, we will all go astray.

PREFACE

That's why I wrote these books, containing insights, observations, and biblical truths distilled over the course of my decades of life and ministry. Each section is designed to be a stand-alone section for study and consideration. I hope this series, *Living Life God's Way*, will be used to disciple men in biblical truths for life. Whether you use it for yourself, with a group, or to mentor or disciple someone else, my hope is that it will be a blessing to you and encourage you to seek God and grow in Him.

HOW TO USE THIS BOOK

What does it mean to be a "good" husband and father?
How do I live out the Christian life at work?
What does God want from me—and how am I supposed to find that out?

These were questions that plagued me as a young man—questions, I learned, that are at the front of many men's minds at various times in their lives. For me, these questions began my quest to seek God and discover the answers, and my discoveries, over the years of my life, led to this series of booklets, *Living Life God's Way*. The series discusses 13 topics that every man must deal with, regardless of his work, calling, profession, or circumstances. It is difficult to know how to live the Christian life without understanding what God says about these areas of life.

These topics are:

1. Seeking and Finding God
2. Who You Are in Christ
3. A Man's Work and Ministry
4. A Man and Authority
5. A Man and His Wife
6. A Man and His Children
7. Getting Guidance from God

8. Overcoming Strongholds
9. A Man and Money
10. Repentance, Forgiveness, and Restitution
11. Being a Leader
12. Sex and Morality
13. The Test of Pride

You can use these books to study on your own, in a small group, or with a larger group of men. Each topic or booklet is a stand-alone study, and a person can begin with any one he chooses. They are different lengths and can be adapted to various settings—home, church, or community—all topics that are pertinent to today.

Explore what the Bible says about these important and critical areas. The encouragement is to read these with an open heart, asking God to reveal His truth to you in each of these areas of life. Pray that His Spirit will show you His truth, so that you may live in it and enjoy all God has for you. I pray that you experience the blessing and presence of God in your life as you draw closer to Him and more aware of His leading in every area of your life.

INTRODUCTION TO BEING A LEADER

When I started my career, I wanted to lead whatever I was involved in. I was wired to lead, so when I was given that position, I took it to heart. God blessed me with leadership roles in national and international companies. I saw Him bless my efforts and felt that I had found my niche.

However, I didn't always lead well. I've made many mistakes in leading and managing others. At times, I've even thought I've made most of the mistakes a leader can make, even though I was trying to lead well and set a good example—I never got up in the morning and said, "I really want to mess up today. I want to make some bad leadership decisions."

So, though I wanted to do a good job, there were things I just had to learn along the way, and other things I had to learn the hard way. I have been fortunate to have some good mentors and some patient bosses.

Leadership is not reserved for a special few. Anyone can learn to lead well. While it is true some are wired or motivated to lead, the basic leadership practices can be learned by anyone who wants to learn them. You don't have to desire to lead a large company or organization to become qualified to lead in your arena.

I believe the Bible teaches that all men are to lead, and that all men can develop the leadership skills to function in the areas to which God has called them. The initial areas we can lead in are in the home, in the workplace, and in the Church.

In the home, a man can learn to lead his family in a manner that pleases God. Since God charges men to do this, it is something all men can learn to do. Beyond these, there are many other areas to lead, such as the political realm, school boards, and other social arenas. However, the basic areas of home, work, and church abound with opportunities to learn and practice leadership.

Leading doesn't always mean being in charge. We don't have to be in charge to lead. A person can show leadership by saying the right thing at the right time, by speaking the truth. Being a good example is showing leadership to others. Doing what God would have us to do is leading, regardless of the circumstances.

In this study, we will look at the responsibility God has given all men to lead. We will then look at how to begin leading where we are, in our present circumstances, in order to fulfill that responsibility. We will also discuss leading others and organizations. We will look at this topic from both a spiritual and practical perspective. Let's jump in!

Chapter 1

QUALITIES OF GODLY LEADERSHIP

Leadership is about getting things done by providing direction to others. A person can lead a small group, a large group, their family members, or simply themself. Leadership is not magic: it is a practical skill that anyone can learn.

In this study, we will look at things a person can do to become a good leader. Some people naturally gravitate to leadership, but they still must learn how to lead effectively. Others may not seek leadership, but they find themselves needing to get tasks done and to display leadership. This study should not just be started but also completed. It is full of practical things a person can do to be an effective leader.

There are qualities that those being led look for their leaders to display, all of which can be developed or learned by those being called on to lead. With practice and through seeking the Lord to teach us these things, a person can become a good or even great leader. Below are some qualities a leader should have and display so others will want to follow. Let's look at some of them.

1. **Courage**: A leader needs to show courage in guiding others to get a job done. This doesn't mean a leader never has doubts or even fear: it means a leader works through those things and has the courage to move ahead. Those who are following him want him to show courage. It gives others around him courage to move forward with him or her and get their part of the job done. There are many examples in Scripture of leaders showing courage and moving forward in faith, obeying God, and seeing great results. One example is found in 1 Samuel 30.

   This chapter tells of David returning to his home in Ziklag, where he was living and leading among the Philistines. He was leading 600 men, all residents of Israel, who were warriors whom God had brought to him. At this time, he and his men were living in a Philistine-controlled city to avoid being killed by King Saul of Israel. The Philistines were preparing to go into battle against King Saul and the Israelites, and the Philistine king whom David served expected him to also go into the battle and fight against the Israelites. God moved upon the various leaders to oppose David going into battle with them, as they feared he might turn against them during the battle and side with his own people. He was told to return to Ziklag. This was God keeping David out of the battle against his own people. But as he and his men returned home, they found that the Amalekites had raided their city and taken all of their wives, children, and goods. They had overcome the city and burned it with fire. The Amalekites killed no one but took them all as captives.

   David and his men were overcome with grief and discouragement. The Bible says they all wept until they had no further strength to weep (that's a lot of hard weeping). The men, who had been with David for years and followed his leadership, now blamed David and spoke of stoning him (throwing rocks at him until he was dead). Not a good way to die!

The Bible says the men were bitter in soul. When bitterness overcomes a person, they are not thinking logically. These men were not thinking logically about the man who had faithfully led them for several years and whom God had anointed to lead them. They were reacting to their circumstances and allowing Satan to influence them to want to kill their godly leader. Scripture states David was "greatly distressed" by this turn of events. But then, David did what a leader does when in a dire circumstance. He had grieved and was distressed, and things looked somewhat hopeless. But the Bible says, *"David strengthened himself in the Lord his God"* (1 Samuel 30:6).

When all seemed lost, David put his grief and distress aside and turned to God for the answer. He summoned his courage and sought God. David called for Abiathar the priest and said, "Bring me the ephod" (a way God was sought in the Old Testament). David then asked God for direction. He asked if he should pursue the Amalekites to recover his and his men's wives, children, and goods. The Lord answered, *"Pursue, for you shall surely overtake and shall surely rescue"* (1 Samuel 30:8). In a time when David could have run to hide, he sought God and went on the offense. He chose to seek and trust God.

So David and his men set out, overtook the Amalekites, defeated them, recovered all that had been taken from them, and also obtained a great amount of goods, or spoil, the Amalekites had taken from numerous sources and cities.

It was a great victory! What looked like defeat turned into a substantial victory from God. David showed great courage in the face of a potential great defeat, and God worked through him to obtain a great victory! This is what a leader needs to do. Seek God and find out God's leadership and direction. Then, obey and watch God work.

2. **Wisdom:** Wisdom means knowing what to do. A person may have knowledge of the circumstances, but they still need wisdom to know what to do or how to use that knowledge to lead others. A great biblical example of wisdom is Solomon. The Bible states he was the wisest man to have lived on the earth. Many might say, "I cannot live up to the wisdom of Solomon." You don't have to. But we must understand where that wisdom came from and that we have that source of wisdom available to us.

   In 1 Kings 3, Solomon went to Gibeon to offer sacrifices to God. Gibeon was the great high place where sacrifices were offered prior to Solomon building the temple in Jerusalem. After Solomon offered his sacrifices to God, the Lord came to Solomon in a dream and asked him what he desired from Him. Solomon asked for wisdom to govern the people of Israel. God was pleased that Solomon asked for wisdom instead of riches, power, or long life. He answered and told Solomon He would grant what he asked for in an abundant manner. He told Solomon that wisdom would be granted to him so that none who lived before him or after him would have the wisdom that He would grant him. So the wisdom came from God.

   James 1:5 states, *"If any of you lacks wisdom, let him ask God, who gives generously to all without reproach, and it will be given him."* This is a great promise. The meaning of this needs to be meditated upon. God says He will give wisdom "generously to all without reproach." The Greek word for *reproach* in this verse comes from the verb *oneidízo*. It translates to mean "cast insults." The word "reproach" is defined in *Webster's Dictionary*, published in 1828 (often more accurate than today's dictionaries), as "shame or disgrace." In other words, God will give wisdom to us generously and will not impart any shame or disgrace because we asked. He wants us to admit we need His leadership and wisdom. There is no shame in our admitting that or asking Him for the wisdom we need. He wants us to have wisdom and will give it freely to us when we ask. So, Solomon's source of wisdom was God. God has much more wisdom than Solomon and wants to give it to us as we need it and when we ask Him for it.

So, a leader needs wisdom to know what to do and when to do it. A godly leader prays and seeks God for wisdom in whatever tasks God gives him. God wants to freely show us how to achieve what He has called us to do. His wisdom is endless, and He says He will give it to us.

3. **Action:** A leader must be a person of action when it comes to making decisions, establishing direction, and getting things done. It doesn't mean he will never make mistakes. If he does make a bad decision or mistake and he realizes it, a good leader will confess that and change course. But a leader acts.

    It's hard to lead when you do nothing. In fact, it's hard to accomplish much at all if you do little or nothing. Wanting something does not get it. Working toward the goal gets things done. With that said, we want to be led by God, seeking His direction and doing the things He is leading us to do. It may be in your job, starting your own business, or obeying Him in reaching out to others and ministering to them (meeting their needs). Obviously, He cannot bless our work if we are doing something that is not His will for us. But discovering His will is not a deep secret we cannot obtain. As we saw above, He desires to give us direction and wisdom. He just wants us to surrender to Him in our hearts, seek Him, and obey His leading.

The Bible states in Matthew 7:7–11:

> *"Ask, and it will be given to you; seek, and you will find; knock, and it will be opened to you. For everyone who asks receives, and the one who seeks finds, and to the one who knocks it will be opened. Or which one of you, if his son asks him for bread, will give him a stone? Or if he asks for a fish, will give him a serpent? If you then, who are evil, know how to give good gifts to your children, how much more will your Father who is in heaven give good things to those who ask Him!"*

God promises to give us direction when we seek Him for it. And since all believers are not evil but His children, He desires to give us, His children, direction.

So leaders must lead and be people who get things done. God will help you in all you do.

4. **Integrity:** Leaders must have integrity for their leadership to bear fruit and for others to want to follow them in the long term. People want to deal with, and work for, people they can trust. Part of being a person of integrity is keeping our word.

   Jesus says in Matthew 5:33–37:

   > *"You shall not swear falsely, but shall perform to the Lord what you have sworn. But I say to you,*

> *do not take an oath at all, either by heaven, for it is the throne of God, or by the earth, for it is His footstool, or by Jerusalem, for it is the city of the great King. And do not take an oath by your hair, for you cannot make one hair white or black. Let what you say be simply 'Yes' or 'No'; anything more than this comes from evil."*

Jesus is saying to act in integrity. Be a person of your word. If there is an acceptable reason why you cannot do as you have said you would, go to the person and explain it to them, and ask to be let out of your commitment to them. Be honest in all of your dealings, and you will have a reputation that others will want to deal with. Integrity begins in the heart. A person of true integrity is honest with himself and honest with God. So, opening your heart to God, being honest with Him, and acting with integrity toward everyone is a sign you are wanting to please God in all you do.

5. **Diligence:** Diligence is an important life quality to have. In our character, we want to be diligent. *Webster's Dictionary*, the 1828 version, states that diligence is the steady and constant application of oneself to accomplish what is undertaken. It is done with care and attention to the task. A diligent person does not let unnecessary delay keep them from working toward a goal. They are not lazy, but industrious in their undertakings. One of the Greek words used that translates into diligence is *spoudé*. It means "haste" or "earnestness." So, a diligent person is reliable and you can count on them to do their best to accomplish their tasks. They take on the task and work diligently to get it done. Another way to show diligence is by persistence. A persistent person is one who does not give up on things that need to be done.

People like to see leaders who have a strong work ethic. Some leaders only want to watch others work and do as little as possible themselves. A good leader knows to work on their own tasks with diligence. People will want to follow those who have a good grasp of the task before them, know how to organize the work to be done, and do the work they need to do. Many tasks are a team effort—they are too great for just one person. Good leaders learn when to delegate and lead others as part of getting the job done. But regardless of the type of task, a good leader shows diligence and personally works to make sure it gets completed.

Proverbs 13:4 states, *"The soul of the sluggard craves and gets nothing, while the soul of the diligent is richly supplied."*

Proverbs 21:5 states, *"The plans of the diligent lead surely to abundance, but everyone who is hasty comes only to poverty."*

The hasty want get-rich-quick schemes and put forth little effort. The diligent complete their work and see the reward. Diligence in one's work will lead to success and blessing.

6. **Communication:** It is important to communicate with family the things they need to know. Communicating the truth is of utmost importance so your family will be based on the truth of God's Word and understand it. Before a man can communicate truth to his family, he must know the truth himself. There is no substitute for seeking God and studying His Word. If you are single, then this is the time to seek God, read His Word, and grow in truth. Become established in the truth of God, and base your life upon it.

In our work, it is important to communicate with others as needed. A good leader communicates with those he is leading and makes sure all are clear on the work they are to do. Also, an important part of communication is to tell others how to improve their work or to let them know if their work is not adequate. This is not always a pleasant part of leading, but it is a necessary one. Some avoid teaching or correcting others altogether to their own and their workers' detriment. This will be discussed in more detail later, but for now, know that correction is a part of leading. Teaching and correction can be done in a positive and constructive manner that benefits all involved.

You don't have to be a great orator to communicate effectively. Just open your mouth and talk, and speak what needs to be said in a positive and truthful manner. If you feel your communication skills are weak, just start communicating and they will improve. Communication is very important. Others are not mind readers and cannot know your thoughts, intentions, or your heart unless you tell them.

Proverbs 29:18 states, *"Where there is not vision, the people perish."*

"Giving vision" means giving direction and an understanding of what needs to be done so your employees or helpers know where they are headed. A good leader needs to do this.

7. **Servant's Heart:** I personally have had to work through this concept to better understand it. Having a servant's heart doesn't mean you do all of the work. It means you are committed to doing what needs to be done. If you have to do it yourself, you do it because your heart is one to serve the needs of others. We serve when we lead because we are accomplishing what needs to be done for all concerned.

Jesus washed His disciples' feet. But He also taught them, corrected them, admonished them, rebuked them, and led them. He did whatever was needed to disciple them and lead them in the way they should go. When He taught them, He was serving their need. When He rebuked or corrected them, He was serving their need. When He encouraged them, He was serving their need. Everything He did, He did with a heart to do what was needed in order to lead them. He did not do it to gain fame, prestige, or honor. He did it because it was needed. That is what a servant does: what is needed. There are many more biblical examples of this.

In Matthew 23:12, Jesus said, "*The greatest among you shall be your servant. Whoever exalts himself will be humbled, and whoever humbles himself will be exalted.*"

In Mark 9:33–37, Jesus asked the disciples:

> "'What were you discussing on the way?' But they kept silent, for on the way they had argued with one another about who was the greatest. And He sat down and called the twelve. And He said to them, 'If anyone would be first, he must be the last of all and servant of all.' And He took a child and put him in the midst of them, and taking him in His arms, He said to them, 'Whoever receives one such child in My name receives Me, and whoever receives Me, receives not Me but him who sent Me.'"

Jesus was dealing with their attitudes and their hearts. So a leader must have a heart to serve others in whatever way is needed and appropriate.

8. **Loyalty:** A leader must be loyal to those serving him and to his family and friends. His workers must know he has their back and will stick with them and support them. Who wants to follow someone who will turn on them and desert them in their hour of need? No one wants to.

Proverbs 17:17 says, *"A friend loves at all times, and a brother is born for adversity."*

I think that states it. We support those we need to support and are loyal to them.

These are character qualities that can be developed, and need to be developed, by leaders. Whether in ministry, in business, at home, in politics, or in any field of work, these are good qualities to pursue.

One thing I want to stress: There is no preferred personality for good or great leadership. Most of us have a stereotype of leadership personality in mind that we have developed for some reason. Many people think of a "Type A" or "Type 1" personality as the one that is successful in leadership—that is, someone who is a good communicator and naturally leads others, a person who is outgoing and strong in personality.

But good or great leadership is learned, and all types of personalities can become good or great leaders. People who by nature are quieter, as well as people who by nature are more outgoing, have made good or great leaders. Your personality is not the litmus test for developing into a leader. Applying yourself and seeking God for His leadership in this is the key. Many people think they are good leaders but actually are lacking. Others who discount themselves are really good leaders in the making. So you, regardless of your personality, past mistakes, or shortcomings, can be a good or great leader.

We may have a vision for our life. We may want to achieve certain things or feel God has given us a task and vision to accomplish. We should start realizing that we do not start at the top. We start where we can—and that may be at the bottom.

Mark 4:26–29 says, *"The kingdom of God is as if a man should scatter seed on the ground, and should sleep by night and rise by day, and the seed should sprout and grow, he himself does not know how.*

For the earth yields crops by itself: first the blade, then the head, after that the full grain in the head. But when the grain ripens, immediately He puts in the sickle, because the harvest has come."

There is a valuable truth in these verses. We sow seeds of effort and trust God to bring the increase. We start to work at the level we have, and the harvest will come over time as it can. The crop comes a step at a time. *First the blade, then the head, and after that, the full grain in the head.* We do not start at the top but learn to be faithful where we are. The vision for our life will come a step at a time as we are faithful.

The Bible says as we gather "little by little," we will become rich:

"Wealth gained quickly will dwindle away, but the one who gathers it little by little will become rich" (Proverbs 13:11).

"Do not despise this small beginning, for the eyes of the Lord rejoice to see the work begin" (Zechariah 4:10).

We may start small, but by being faithful to our work and seeking God to direct our steps, we will increase and eventually the vision will come to pass. Don't despise small beginnings. Seek God, work, be faithful, and watch what He does over time. Most great enterprises have been built over time with effort and faithfulness.

Let's look at a great example of leadership the Bible gives in Nehemiah.

QUESTIONS FOR REFLECTION AND DISCUSSION:

1. Do you feel a bit overwhelmed by the prospect of trying to become a good or great leader?

   _____
   _____
   _____
   _____

2. Do you have confidence that God will help you to develop the skills, aptitudes, and qualities you need to accomplish the things He wants you to accomplish?

   _____
   _____
   _____
   _____

3. The question really is, "Will God help to get the things done He wants me to?". He promises He will and will lead you along the way if you seek Him and ask Him to. Are you willing to start taking the responsibility to lead in the areas God wants you to?

   _____
   _____
   _____
   _____

4. Do you get discouraged at the results you are accomplishing? What have you learned in this first chapter about being faithful and believing God will bless your efforts?

_____
_____
_____
_____

TAKE A KNEE

Let's kneel before God and pray. If you are unable to kneel physically, then kneel in your heart.

Dear Lord, help me to obey You to take on the responsibilities You desire me to take on. Help me to take leadership of myself and to lead others as You prompt or lead me to. Thank You that You are always with me and will never forsake me. I know I can count on You to give me the wisdom I need and show me how to accomplish all You want me to do.

Chapter 2

What Is Leadership?

He was one man, with a giant task.

The man arose during the night, when others were asleep, to survey the job that lay ahead. The city of his fathers lay decimated. The protective wall had been torn down, and was surrounded by other cities filled with people who did not want to see that city restored, and who were prepared to use force if necessary to stop any progress. The inhabitants of the city, his people, felt defeated and discouraged. It could be a very difficult task, and all the odds seemed to be against him.

But in his heart, the man believed God had given him a task to do: rebuild the wall and restore the city. In addition, he felt compelled to re-establish the worship of God in this city. It was a great task, and he realized he would need God's anointing on him and His leadership to get it done.

Prior to this, the man had enjoyed a very influential position in the court of a king in a distant land, a king whom he had closely and personally served. It was a trusted position with direct access to the king daily. Over time, the king grew to trust him and value him. He had a good life and likely could have been very happy and comfortable there for the rest of his life.

But God had put on his heart that he had a job to do. He was to go back to the city of His people—Jerusalem—and restore it. His people—the Jews—had been conquered by Babylon and the city destroyed decades before. But God had promised to restore the city in the proper time. In recent years, a contingent of Jews had gone back to Jerusalem to rebuild the temple, but the protective wall lay in ruins and the city was struggling. The man believed this was the time, and that he was the one to take on the task.

Without supernatural help, it seemed an impossible task. But the desire would not go away. It burned inside him until he became convinced he was to boldly step out. One day, as he served the king, the king noticed his countenance was different. His normal cheerful nature was not there; there was something wrong. So the king asked him, "Why is your face sad though you are not sick? This is nothing but sadness of heart."

The man was afraid to answer. If he displeased the king, all could be lost, including his position and his dream. He gathered his courage and replied, "Let the king live forever. Why should my face not be sad when the city, the place of my fathers' tombs, lies desolate and its gates have been consumed by fire?"

There. He had said it. Now, with great anticipation, he awaited the king's reply. The king said, "What would you request?"

The man silently prayed to God for favor, and he replied, "If it please the king, and if your servant has found favor before you, send me to Judah, to the city of my fathers' tombs, that I may rebuild it." He again waited anxiously for the reply.

The king said, "How long will your journey be, and when will you return?"

The man could hardly believe his ears. Was this was really happening? What God had put in his heart was becoming reality. He realized God was granting him favor. Now he boldly asked, "If it please the king, let letters be given me for the governors of the provinces beyond the River, that they may allow me to pass through until I come to Judah, and a letter to Asaph the keeper of the king's forest, that he may give me timber to make beams for the gates of the fortress which is by the temple, for the wall of the city and for the house to which I will go."

To the man's great surprise and delight, the king granted all he asked for. The king made him the governor of Jerusalem, gave him the provisions he needed, and blessed his mission. God's favor was with him. Now the task had begun. The dream phase had turned into the "get it done" phase. It was time to size up the situation, look at the assets available to do the job, organize it all, and go to work. And, oh yes, lead it all from start to finish! It would take faith and real leadership skills to accomplish the dream.

This is the story of Nehemiah. You can read it in your Bible in Nehemiah chapter 2. This man had been a captive from the conquest of the kingdom of Judah by the Babylonians. He, along with some other capable Jews, had attained prominent positions under the various kings to help preserve the Jewish people in captivity.

Nehemiah became the king's cup bearer. He would taste all beverages intended for the king to make sure they had not been poisoned. In this position, he risked his life for the king daily. He had access to the king regularly, and the king came to know the kind of person Nehemiah was, and respected him.

But it was his faith in God that motivated Nehemiah. God put in him a desire to return to Jerusalem to rebuild and re-establish the city. But how would he do that? Miraculously, the king granted all he needed.

But even after the king blessed him to go and he arrived in Jerusalem, as he viewed the size of the task, he realized the job that lay ahead was monumental. Thankfully, God put a plan in his heart. Nehemiah shared this with the people in Jerusalem and they rallied around him. God supernaturally moved on their hearts to follow Nehemiah and caused them to believe the plan was of Him. They knew they needed to follow Nehemiah and his plan.

Nehemiah organized all of the people and gave each a part to play. Despite outright hostility and opposition from neighboring cities and nations, they finished the wall in 55 days, a job that could have easily taken a year or more. Nehemiah then set about to re-establish the temple worship and turn the hearts of the people back to God. He proved to be a great leader with an obedient heart and determination to follow God. He had faith that God was leading him and would help him accomplish the task.

What gave this man his faith, vision, and resolute heart to accomplish God's plan for him? He believed and trusted God. His task would challenge every part of his being; his faith, his convictions, his determination, his ability to lead and keep others on course, and his trust in God.

> *Dreams and desires turn into tasks that*
> *often are larger than you imagined,*
> *with problems, difficulties, and challenges along the way.*
> *But if it is of God, it will work out. He will enable you.*

Many people think of a leader as the person in charge, the one who makes decisions and tells others what to do. Depending on one's experiences with leaders, there may be good or bad associations with the word. However, in this study our focus is on leadership as we see it in the Bible. From a task perspective, it is the leader's job to get the task completed. We will see this in our study of Nehemiah. He was an effective leader that got the job done.

From a leadership style perspective, the way the leader leads will have an impact on those he is leading, either positive or negative. He may get the job done, but how has he impacted those working with him?

Then there is the culture the leader works to establish in his organization or group. The culture is the way his workers relate to each other and to the leader. It is whether or not those working with the leader like coming to work, whether or not they believe in the leader and his ability or lead. Whether or not they enjoy working with him and their fellow workers. Is there an atmosphere of trust, of mutual respect, and a feeling of safety rather than fear or intimidation?

These three things—effectiveness, leadership style, and workplace culture—are all things on which the leader has a great impact. During this study, we will touch on all of these. First, let's look at how a leader is effective to get things done.

Demonstrates the initiative to take care of and take charge of the responsibilities, people, or situations God has entrusted to him or her. Further, they give direction to those who are helping them in those efforts.

To lead we must do just that—lead. And regardless of our circumstances, we can show leadership. Think of leading as taking initiative and getting things done. If others are under our leadership, then as a leader we must also:

1. organize
2. give direction

3. determine what to take responsibility for and the things others should do
4. delegate the tasks to be accomplished by others
5. manage the process
6. be responsible for the outcome

There is one thing we need to take note of. Nehemiah was not a priest or a religious leader when God put on his heart the job He had for him. In fact, almost all of the people in the Bible God chose to accomplish things were not priests or religious leaders. They were simply willing people through whom God wanted to work. God moved on them and they obeyed—however, not always willingly.

You see, many of them had the reservations we have. They did not feel qualified. They didn't feel capable. They were unsure they could get the job done.

Actually, they couldn't get the job done. But God could, working through them. God often did not pick qualified people. Instead, He picked willing people to get big things done, people through whom He could work, very imperfect people who submitted themselves to His will.

It's the same today. God is looking for people He can work through, not the most talented or most qualified. Just willing vessels, submitted to Him.

Faithful with a Trust

Our lives, our responsibilities, and our possessions are gifts God has entrusted to us. The Bible teaches that as we learn to be faithful over what God has given us, it causes us to grow both spiritually and practically.

> *He who is faithful in what is least is faithful also in much; and he who is unjust in what is least is unjust also in much.*

Therefore if you have not been faithful in the unrighteous mammon, who will commit to your trust the true riches? And if you have not been faithful in what is another man's, who will give you what is your own? (Luke16:10-12, NKJV)

Those who learn to be faithful over small things develop the skills and character to be entrusted with more. In addition, if we are not faithful in practical areas, such as our time, resources, home, work, money, and material items, how can we be trusted with more?

Faithfulness in practical matters develops character that allows us to be faithful over greater responsibilities, both practical and spiritual. God wants to use all men and women in His kingdom. Part of His plan is to develop us into the people He wants us to be so He can use us as He has planned. He works *in* us so that He can be released in our lives in a greater manner and then work *through* us.

The parable of the talents in Matthew 25:14-30 speaks of this. In this parable, the word *talent* refers to a measurement of money. Obviously, we should be responsible stewards of everything God has given us, not only money.

Jesus told the story of three servants who were given different amounts of money to use while their master went away. When the master returned, he asked for an accounting. What did they accomplish? What were the results of their efforts?

Two servants acted wisely and multiplied what he had entrusted to them. Obviously, they had to take initiative, use wisdom, and apply themselves diligently to do this. They had to take risks, work hard, and take the steps to make things work out. They had to do their part. Over time, they likely developed valuable character qualities such as a good work ethic, dealing fairly and in integrity with others, so others would want to do business with them, and with an awareness of opportunities around them.

They did not just sit around and dream about what could happen; they established direction and worked at making it happen. These men did not double the talents overnight. Such a task might have taken months or years. The Bible states the master returned "after a long time." The two faithful servants did not take the attitude, *He will be gone for a long time. I can rest and take it easy for awhile.* No, they took on the task, they were diligent, and their results impressed their master.

The third servant was fearful and took no initiative to use what had been given to him. He simply buried it in the ground until his master returned. The master praised the ones who used his capital wisely, applied themselves, and multiplied the money he had given them. He condemned the one who did not try, and did nothing. Notice in the story he called the third servant "wicked and lazy." That seems a bit harsh. Why not give the guy a break and give him credit for at least not losing it? After all, the master did get his money back.

What's important here is that the Bible says the master gave to each man according to his ability. The one-talent guy had the ability to manage one talent but didn't. He didn't even try. The talent was a trust given to the servant. The man turned out to be lazy and put no effort into trying to fulfill his master's instructions. He gave no value to the opportunity he had been given. He was disobedient, disrespectful of his master, and ungrateful. He even tried to blame his behavior on his master by saying the reason he gave no effort was because he was afraid he could not please his master. He said, "I knew you were a hard man, harvesting where you have not sown and gathering where you have not scattered seed. So I was afraid and went out and hid your talent in the ground."

He was essentially saying, "I knew I could not please you, so why try?" He was saying to the master, "It is really your fault I did not try. If you had been a better master, maybe I would have tried harder." The master had given him a gift and a great opportunity to change his life and obtain great reward. But he did nothing, and blamed his bad attitudes, his lack of trying, and his laziness on his master. He would not accept any responsibility for his lack of effort. Obviously the other servants did not feel this way. They grasped the opportunity with enthusiasm.

The master looked at the lazy servant's heart and called him wicked because of his attitudes and actions. No respect, no effort, no results. Many try to paint a picture of God as harsh and difficult to please. But the Bible states He is a loving God who delights in helping and guiding us as we seek Him.

For a reward, the master gave the faithful stewards cities to govern. Their faithfulness over what they had been given—and the character qualities and action they demonstrated—qualified them to be responsible for even more. He showed he was a generous man who rewarded faithfulness. He was not the man the unprofitable servant accused him of being.

The principle here is that as we are faithful over what we have been given, we develop skills, knowledge, and positive character traits. The interesting thing is that these men were given cities to rule over. The Bible says we, as followers of Christ, will rule and reign with Jesus (see 1 Corinthians 6:2-3; 2 Timothy 2:12; Revelation 20:6) . In this life, God is preparing us to live successfully and also preparing us for the next life with Him.

The basis of becoming a good leader is developing the inner qualities that will make us good leaders.

The Bible says God is committed to developing Christlike character in us: *"Being confident of this very thing, that He who has begun a good work in you will complete it until the day of Jesus Christ"* (Philippians 1:6).

In his epistle to the Colossians, the apostle Paul wrote that he and Timothy were *"warning every man and teaching every man in all wisdom, that we may present every man perfect in Christ Jesus"* (Colossians 1:28). The Amplified version says, *". . . that we may present every person mature (full-grown, fully initiated, complete, and perfect) in Christ (the Anointed One)."* God is working in us to become more like Christ, to make us mature, and He wants to develop us to be productive in this life. He wants to work through us to accomplish the things He desires.

Faithful Where We Are

God desires all of us to develop positive, practical, and useful character traits, no matter what our circumstances. Most men either have some type of work to do, a family, or both. The everyday work world and home life are areas where we can begin to show faithfulness. Even if a man is single and unemployed, he can still show initiative and diligence by establishing disciplines of seeking God and being diligent to look for work.

Let's consider some practical ways to take faithful initiative with what God has entrusted to you.

In the home . . .
- Arrange schedules so there is regular family time.
- Teach your children biblical truths and character traits. Teach them about God and His nature. Tell them He loves them and has good plans for their lives.
- Spend regular quality time with your wife and children. Talk to them, listen to them, and love them.
- Plan family vacations and family time together.
- Keep the home and property in good repair and well maintained.

- Keep the cars in good repair and clean.
- Take your family to church and get involved.
- Teach your family to help others.
- Supervise your children's activities.
- Manage your family finances and financial affairs.
- Provide interesting Bible studies/discussions of spiritual things (at a level suitable for your children).
- Pray for your family, and pray regularly with your wife and children.

At work . . .

- Take initiative to get things done and done well.
- Do all you do to the best of your ability. Go the extra mile.
- Learn all you can about your work. Be an expert at what you do.
- Get things done on time.
- Be responsive and reliable. Return phone calls and emails promptly.
- Maintain a positive attitude. Be cheerful.
- Support and show respect to those in authority over you.
- Be punctual.
- Treat others with respect. Do not be critical of your fellow workers. Refuse to participate in gossip or being critical of others.
- Use honesty and integrity in all of your dealings.
- Pray over your work and your workplace. Pray for those in authority over you. Ask God for wisdom and insight into your work (see 1 Timothy 2:1-3; Romans 13:1-5).
- Study the book of Proverbs and take note of the many truths contained in this book regarding the workplace and daily life.

Diligence, integrity, faithfulness, initiative, discipline, and relational skills are all building blocks to being a good leader. Whether we have a little or a lot, whether we aspire to be a leader or not, God desires us to develop these character traits. The goal is not to be faithful just to get more, but to do so because that is what God desires us to do.

We should view our workplace as the place where God has put us, where He wants us to have a positive influence on the lives of those around us. Our ministry in our workplace is to be a person who is a light, with the life of Christ in us. We do this by our example of how we work, our attitudes, and how we live our life in front of those around us.

Some people seem to be born with an inclination to lead. They want to lead and may thrive in leadership roles. The question is, are they good leaders? Have they built the character and skills to make them effective? Those who are given responsibility over others but have never learned responsibility for themselves will flounder.

Even if you do not have a natural desire to lead others or have a position leading others, the Lord still wants you to take responsibility for yourself and for what He has given you. That is the foundation of leadership. Leadership is not something to be afraid of or feel incompetent about. Simply focus on being faithful. This will develop godly character that will allow God to use you according to His purposes.

Discovering and yielding to God's plan and purpose for us should be our goal. How does He want to use us? What does He want us to accomplish? As we focus on faithfulness and are open to God's leading, His plan will unfold.

As a young man, an older man who took an interest in me challenged me to learn to lead my family. He taught me that leading was not giving orders, but learning to love my wife and children, caring for them, teaching them about God's will for them by example, and communicating biblical truth to them.

My children are now grown and I have grandchildren, and I am still learning how to do that. But I am thankful I was challenged to begin this as a young man. I needed to learn a lot, but as I sought God He helped me.

Next, we are going to look at how God develops leaders. Then we are going to focus on practical ways to lead.

QUESTIONS FOR REFLECTION AND DISCUSSION

1. What are three ways in which you take responsibility for yourself?

2. List the areas you believe God has given you to be faithful over.

3. As you consider your initiative and responsibility in these areas, what is going well? Is there an area in which you would like to improve or a problem you are struggling to solve?

_____

_____

_____

_____

TAKE A KNEE

Let's kneel before God and pray. If you are unable to kneel, then kneel to God in your heart. *"Dear Father, I realize You want me to be faithful and to learn to be an effective steward over what you have given me—my time, my money and resources, my family, my responsibilities, as well as all of my relationships. Begin to show me how to be more effective and faithful. I may make mistakes at times, but I realize You love me. You are always there to restore me, teach me, train me, and correct me because I am Your son. You delight for me to seek You and seek Your wisdom. I also realize You delight to see me grow in character. I invite You to be involved in all areas of my life. Give me wisdom and understanding. Thank You for Your love and faithfulness."*

Chapter 3

God's School of Leadership

Sam naturally gravitated toward leading. He worked hard and wanted to do a good job. He was mentally bright and had natural abilities that led to leadership positions. However, a character issue continually undermined his efforts. He was critical and proud. He found fault with others and analyzed their weaknesses—he actually thought that was one of the primary things a leader was supposed to do.

Rather than encouraging others and building them up, he wanted to point out their shortcomings. There is a time for dealing with shortcomings when needed. But to make others feel like you are always looking for their weaknesses and are anxious to point them out does not promote good and positive relationships.

He tried to boost himself by being critical of others and boasting of his successes and self-perceived good qualities. At times he offended people, which caused those under his leadership to lose confidence in him.

Even though they recognized his abilities, those in authority over him were reluctant to entrust more to him. They were unsure of his judgment and the effect he might have on others. As a result, his career stagnated. He wanted to advance, but his critical nature and pride hurt him and kept him back. Since Sam was a Christian, this was an enigma that hurt him.

Dennis was a man of energy. He had a reputation of being diligent and trying to excel in all he did. Additional qualities set him apart. First, he was humble and was always trying to build up others. He was quick to compliment and give credit to others and maintained a cheerful and positive attitude. He was not only well liked, but also admired for his efforts, abilities, and attitude.

When the time came to appoint a person for a significant leadership position, Dennis was chosen over others who were older and more experienced. He had won the confidence of those around him and those in authority over him. People trusted him and his judgment. They believed he would always be fair to those he worked for and to those who worked for him. Yes, he had ability and a good work ethic, but his character and attitudes made him stand out. Dennis was truly a *gifted* leader.

Many schools teach leadership and practical skills and methods of leadership, and some are quite good. I personally have benefitted from such schools. However, God values character first, and His leadership school develops character as a basis for leadership. We see this in the lives of Joseph, Moses, David, Daniel, and others in the Bible. As they responded to God, obeyed Him, and grew in wisdom, God's plan for them continued to unfold. God knew that when their character was ready, they would carry out their responsibilities with a right heart.

Joseph the Leader

Many of us are familiar with the Old Testament account of Joseph. He had a natural desire to lead, and God had even given him dreams of leading. He shared his dreams with his brothers and, since he was younger than they were, they grew angry and jealous of him. They did not like the idea of him ruling over them, which was the implication of the dreams he shared with them. So, when they had the opportunity, they sold him as a slave to get rid of him.

However, God had a plan. He wanted to raise Joseph to a position of leadership over all of Egypt. There, Joseph would not only provide for his family; he would play a key role in God's promise to Abraham to make his descendants a great nation. So God's school of leadership development began. God was developing Joseph into a great leader.

> It would be helpful to stop and read Genesis chapters 37 and 39–41.

Most of us would not choose becoming a slave as a training path to learn to lead. Joseph had come from a wealthy household with a position of favor with his father. Going from a life of plenty and privilege to one of bondage would have caused many to give up.

But while a slave, Joseph chose to trust God and applied himself to his responsibilities, and God blessed his work. Joseph's master was Potiphar, a high-ranking Egyptian, and he recognized Joseph's efforts and appointed him chief steward of his estate.

When Potiphar's wife began to desire him and tried to seduce him, Joseph remained righteous and resisted. The Bible says he ran out of the house to resist the temptation. Because he would not succumb to her repeated advances, she became angry and accused him of trying to rape her. Obviously she was used to getting her way. Potiphar believed his wife and threw Joseph into jail, where his situation seemed to deteriorate. It appeared that doing the right thing made things worse.

Many would say, "Okay, here I've worked hard, been faithful, and tried to do the right thing. Look where it has gotten me. I've gone from becoming a slave to a convict. I've done nothing wrong and this is the reward I get; things are getting worse. This just isn't working for me." Think about it. Joseph was betrayed by his brothers and sold by them into slavery. Then, while working hard and excelling in his work, he was punished for doing right and not betraying his master's trust, and wound up in prison. This would break most men. They would get the "woe-is-me" attitude and want to give up. Maybe they would sulk and want sympathy. Or they might think, "It's time to hide my talent in the sand and give up. I don't think I can please God." But not Joseph.

Joseph continued to trust God and again applied himself to his duties. Now his career path included being a favored son of a wealthy man, then a slave and a prisoner. But again, he was blessed. The head jailer watched him and the abilities and attitudes he demonstrated, and put him in charge of the prison affairs.

Joseph could have given up. He could have developed bad attitudes and blamed God for his state of affairs. Yet he didn't. To me, this is what makes Joseph such an example. I'm sure he was discouraged at times. But Joseph continued to choose to trust God and apply his best efforts.

After a few years, two of Pharaoh's servants were thrown into jail. Each had a dream, and Joseph, through understanding from God's Spirit, interpreted the dreams. Later, Pharaoh himself had a dream that troubled him, and wanted to know its meaning. Pharaoh's servant then remembered Joseph and his ability to interpret dreams and told Pharaoh. Joseph was called in and interpreted the dream. Pharaoh recognized God's hand on Joseph and made him governor over all Egypt. From a prisoner to a ruler with great favor overnight! Only God can do that.

Joseph realized God's plan in His time. Most bible scholars estimate he was sold into slavery at 17, and his time as a slave and prisoner lasted 13 years. That would make him 30 when he was freed from prison and elevated as governor over Egypt.

But God first prepared Joseph for His plan. He developed Joseph's character, changed his heart attitudes, and developed his practical leadership skills over a period of years. God was using Joseph during that time as an example to those around him, but Joseph was being prepared for far greater use. Even in adversity, God was with Joseph—leading him, guiding him, blessing him, and developing him into the man He wanted him to be.

God always has a plan; we simply need to seek Him, trust Him, and cooperate with Him. Since Joseph was human, I'm sure at times he was discouraged. But he continued to choose to trust God. He didn't give up. Even though we may go through hardship and trials, God still has a plan for us. We must seek God for understanding, learn what He is wanting to teach us, submit to His will for us, and keep trusting Him to raise us up at the proper time.

By the way, God does not tell us up front how long our training time will last. It may be a few months or a number of years. But He does tell us to be faithful, to trust Him, and be diligent in our work.

Moses, David, and Daniel

Three other examples of men God used in leadership were Moses, David, and Daniel. When we read about these men, we note that the Bible focuses on their relationships with God as more important than the actual details of their leadership abilities. While all these men were in prominent leadership roles, their success came from their relationships with God. All three experienced great testing and trials; yet all are spoken of as men who chose God and His ways.

Of the three, we have the greatest detail about David. Scripture presents both David's successes and failures as examples to learn from. The lives of Joseph and Daniel are presented almost without fault. While we know they were human and had faults and weaknesses, the accounts the Bible gives of their lives concentrates on their trust in God and their relationship with Him.

We find the following traits among these men. Let's consider them:

- **They studied the Scriptures to discover God's will** (they only had a few of the Bible's books to read, as the majority of the Bible had not yet been written). Moses actually wrote the first five books of the Bible under God's inspiration. So he had to study his own books. It was his relationship with God that set him apart.
- **They prayed about their lives and circumstances**. The Bible says Daniel prayed three times a day (Daniel 6:10). David spoke of rising early in the morning to pray and seek God. He also spoke of praying and seeking God during the night watches. He was obviously a man of prayer. Moses actually spent 40 days and nights fasting, praying, and seeking God—twice! By the way, a person cannot go without water for 40 days. Moses did it twice. It was truly a miracle of God. God supernaturally sustained him! These men sought God's direction regarding their circumstances both under trial and during times of success.
- **They all endured adversity**. During those times, God gave them wisdom and brought them through the difficulty. God also used the adversity to grow them and develop character in their lives.

- **They were obedient to God.** As God gave them understanding of His will or direction, they carried it out and obeyed Him. They were obedient to the direction God gave them and pursued it even when it meant possible personal harm. Because of this, they saw God work in their lives in great and miraculous ways.
- **They were men of action.** They put their understanding of what needed to be done into practical action.
- **They had strong convictions.** They were zealous for God and bold about their beliefs.
- **They sought God for wisdom.** They were known for having great wisdom. This came from seeking God and asking for His wisdom.
- **They were faithful.** Those in authority over them had great confidence in them because of their initiative and character.
- **They were humble towards God.** They had servants' hearts toward Him.
- **They were diligent and faithful in all they did.**

David, Moses, and Daniel all went through times of training, testing, and character development before they came into the fullness of what God had for them. God was always with them, leading and delivering them. He loved them during hardship and failures. Because He is faithful, He brought them through it all and into the fulfillment of His promises. While our lives will not be identical to these men, God may use a similar pattern with us.

Remember, the training times do not mean that God is punishing us or He is displeased with us. He will allow us to be tested. But He never leaves us or forsakes us. He is always with us, loving us and standing ready to teach and strengthen us. God will use us from the time we become Christians. He always wants to work through us, even as He is working in us.

The steps of a good man [all believers who seek Him] are ordered by the Lord, and He delights in his way. Though he fall, he shall not be utterly cast down; for the Lord upholds him with His hand. I have been young, and now am old; yet I have not seen the righteous forsaken, nor his descendants begging bread. He is ever merciful, and lends; and His descendants are blessed. (Psalm 37:23-26; see also Hebrews 13:5)

If you are in a difficult place, God desires you to be willing to trust Him even in these circumstances. This may be a good time to recommit yourself to God and seek His purposes and wisdom in your life. If we ask for wisdom, He promises to answer (James 1:2-6).

God's leadership school is often longer than we might think. He broods over us and works in us to develop the person He sees we can be. He will work both in us and through us as we yield to Him. Few men get placed into the types of positions David, Moses, Daniel, and Joseph were put into. Yet God desires to build His character into all of our lives and has a purpose for all of us. Our responsibility is to seek Him, be faithful, and be obedient.

QUESTIONS FOR REFLECTION AND DISCUSSION

1. Consider an adverse circumstance you have encountered. Did you seek God during those times? If so, how did it affect you spiritually?

   _____
   _____
   _____
   _____

2. In what ways were you able to trust God during that time? In what way did you struggle?

_____
_____
_____
_____

3. How did that time shape your character?

_____
_____
_____
_____

4. What benefits did that time bring you? What did you learn?

_____
_____
_____
_____

TAKE A KNEE

Let's pray: *"Father, if I did not fully learn the things You desired to teach me during any difficult times, please reveal them to me so I can understand. I pray Your Spirit will begin to show me what You want me to know. I want to develop into the person You want me to be. While I realize that adversity can come from Satan, I know You still desire for me to learn and grow during those times. Teach me, train me, and anoint me to accomplish all You have for me. I choose to trust You and seek You, no matter what my circumstances are. Help me to bloom and thrive where I am planted. I thank You that You are faithful and true and will never leave me or forsake me."*

Chapter 4

BIBLICAL QUALIFICATIONS FOR LEADERSHIP

It is interesting that, in the Bible, the qualifications for a leader do not mention talents, abilities, skills or giftings, but rather character qualities or traits. The emphasis is on the person we are and our relationship with God. This emphasis is born out by the story of David. In 1 Samuel 16, we see Samuel being sent by God to ordain the next king of Israel. He was led to the household of Jesse of the tribe of Judah to discover the next man God had chosen to be king.

Jesse had eight sons and the oldest seven passed before Samuel. Samuel thought that the first son, Eliab, was worthy and said to himself, *"Surely this is the man the Lord has chosen."* (Evidently Eliab was an impressive-looking guy.) But God didn't choose him. As Jesse's first seven sons passed before Samuel, none of them were selected. Finally the youngest, David, who was shepherding the flock, was brought in and the Lord told Samuel he was the chosen one.

The Bible tells us, regarding the choosing of David, *"The Lord does not look at the things man looks at. Man looks at the outward appearance, but the Lord looks at the heart"* (1 Samuel 16:7). God values the heart of a man more than his abilities. The heart would be a person's attitudes, the things he holds to be important, his values, the way he thinks, and the way he lives his life. And, most importantly, his heart attitudes toward the Lord.

It's not that abilities are not important; they are. When God chooses someone for a job, He already knows their talents and abilities. But talents and abilities need to be developed to reach their potential. In the same way, a person's character needs to be developed. God is in the character-development business.

Let's consider the character traits the Bible speaks of regarding church leaders. Certainly these are traits God desires for all men. Throughout the Bible, and especially in Proverbs, God speaks of character traits He desires. In 1 Timothy 3 and Titus 1, the apostle Paul outlines character traits that were qualifications for church leadership (I hope you will take a few moments to read these passages.)

Sometimes the qualities we need most are not the ones we think we need. When I was chosen to be an elder in my local church at a fairly young age, we (those who had been selected) were put into office during a special ordination service. During this time, the current elders laid hands on those being put into office and prayed for them. A man I respected laid his hands on me and prayed for me. While he did this, he spoke these words: "Lou, listen more and speak less. Don't be so anxious to speak your opinions. Listen to others."

I am grateful that this man was direct and honest about where I needed to change in order to mature as the leader God wanted me to be. We all have these areas. We have to be open and willing to seek God to change us as He reveals our need to mature.

What might these areas be? There are two key chapters in the New Testament that speak of the character traits God wants us to have. These should be sought by all men, whether or not they are currently church leaders.

Traits in 1 Timothy 3

In the first passage, when writing to Timothy, the apostle Paul instructed:

Therefore an overseer must be above reproach, the husband of one wife, sober-minded, self-controlled, respectable, hospitable, able to teach, not a drunkard, not violent but gentle, not quarrelsome, not a lover of money.

He must manage his own household well, with all dignity keeping his children submissive, for if someone does not know how to manage his own household, how will he care for God's church?

He must not be a recent convert, or he may become puffed up with conceit and fall into the condemnation of the devil.

Moreover, he must be well thought of by outsiders, so that he may not fall into disgrace, into a snare of the devil. (1 Timothy 3:2-7)

In this passage, we see a profile of the kind of man God desires us to be. Let's look at the meaning of these character traits.

"Above reproach." This does not mean a perfect person who never makes mistakes. Rather, this speaks of a man who always purposes to do the right thing. He is willing to admit when he is wrong and does what is necessary to right any wrong. He always

purposes to abstain from wrongdoing. He strives to do all with honesty and integrity.

"The husband of one wife." This man understands that God desires the covenant made at marriage to be for life. His heart is given to one woman, his wife. He cleaves to her, loves her, and is faithful to her. He has a "one-woman" heart for his wife.

"Sober minded." He does not let himself be carried away on a whim, a fad. He does not make rash decisions. He is a realist. He sees things for what they are. He is practical.

"Self-controlled." This man is not given to excess. He does not allow himself to be controlled by addictions, passions, and appetites. He eats, but is not controlled by appetite. He loves, but is not controlled by lust. He does not allow himself to be controlled by any improper substances. He is disciplined and controls his passions. He also controls his anger.

"Respectable." This man behaves himself. He is considerate of others and conducts himself in a manner worthy of respect, with honesty and integrity. He acts in a manner that others would speak well of.

"Hospitable." This man is willing to share his blessings from God. He will open his home to others. More than that, he is cheerful and finds joy in helping others and spending time with others. He has a giving heart and wants to bless others.

"Able to teach." This is not to be confused with one who has the gift of teaching. He knows the Word of God and can share it with others as needed. He may not teach from a pulpit, but is able to teach or communicate truth to his children or others for their benefit.

We can all learn to teach or communicate effectively. For some it will take practice and coaching from our spouses, friends, or mentors. A place to practice teaching is with our children as we teach them right from wrong, honesty, a work ethic, and as we give them other valuable input that they need.

"Not a drunkard." He does not get drunk. He is not addicted to alcohol. He is unwilling to let alcohol cause him to lose control or be guilty of actions under its influence which could harm or hurt others, as well as his own reputation.

"Not violent, but gentle." This does not mean he is a coward or is unwilling to fight if needed. A man can be both gentle and have great courage and boldness. The difference is his motivation. He does not seek violence. He is a peacemaker. Nevertheless, he would lay down his life if necessary to fight for what is right and godly. He is confident but not brash or boastful.

"Not quarrelsome." Some people are not violent, but they have contentious natures. They are always ready to argue and prove their point. They always need to be right. These types of people seem to live in an atmosphere of strife and contention. Valuing relationships and others is more important than always being right. We ought to love others and not to think more highly of ourselves than we should (Romans 12:3)

"Not a lover of money." This man is not greedy and does not compromise his integrity to get gain. Money is a tool we use in life, not something we are to love or crave. A wealthy man is not necessarily a lover of money. A poor man or a wealthy man can be a lover of money.

A person can both be content and work hard. The Bible teaches us to be content if our needs are met (1 Timothy 6:8). But it also teaches us to work and excel in our work (Proverbs 22:29). The driving force of our lives should not be to seek to be wealthy (Proverbs 3:9-10, 23:4-5). If God blesses our work and we have great gain, so be it. However, we obtain it through our work and God's blessing. We do not live just to make more money. We live to please the Lord and enjoy what He has given us.

We labor in faith that He will bless our work, but are content along the way. This is a condition of our heart. Can we be ambitious for our work to prosper and yet be content at the same time? Yes. We can have goals for our work or business to prosper and be successful, but be content in our personal life with our needs met. We should ask God to do that work in our heart—wanting all God has for us, but being content along the way. Contentment is based on our relationship with God, not with how much money we have.

"One who rules his own house well, having his children in submission with all reverence." To be a leader in the church, a man must have his own house in order. There is a reason for this: *"For if a man does not know how to rule his own house, how will he take care of the church of God?"* (1 Timothy 3:5).

Since he is the leader of his home, he should demonstrate that he leads well there. His relationships with his wife and his children are very important. His children being in submission means they have been taught to respect him and authority. He is not harsh with his children or else they will likely be in rebellion and live in fear. Rather, he loves his children and they know he loves them. He teaches them and encourages, admonishes, and corrects his children in love.

In addition, his residence should be in order. If his house is a mess and is not a credit to his neighborhood, then he has a bad witness. It doesn't need to be lavish or luxurious, but clean, neat, and as well maintained as he has the means to do.

"Not a novice." New believers are not to be put into positions of church leadership. They are untested and could be tempted to get caught up in pride. A novice could also lack the wisdom to carry out the office of a church leader. Before a person can be an elder, he must demonstrate the character and wisdom needed for that position. Those who have been through trials and times

of testing and discouragement, and have chosen to trust God through those times, are men who have been tested.

"Must have a good reputation with those who are outside." This man lives his convictions seven days a week. He pays his bills on time, deals fairly with others, and has a good reputation in the community. He is a man of honesty and integrity. He is compassionate and shows mercy toward others.

Traits in Titus 1

The second key passage is found when the apostle Paul wrote to Titus, giving directions for his ministry on the island of Crete. Paul gave instructions for the kind of men to appoint as elders in "every town":

> *If anyone is above reproach, the husband of one wife, and his children are believers and not open to the charge of debauchery or insubordination. For an overseer, as God's steward, must be above reproach. He must not be arrogant or quick-tempered or a drunkard or violent or greedy for gain, but hospitable, a lover of good, self-controlled, upright, holy, and disciplined. He must hold firm to the trustworthy word as taught, so that he may be able to give instruction in sound doctrine and also to rebuke those who contradict it.* (Titus 1:6-9)

We have already seen some of these characteristics from 1 Timothy. Let's consider the additional characteristics Paul mentioned.

"Not arrogant." The meaning here for arrogance is "self-pleasing" or "self-willed." This is a tough one. We all are self-willed at times. But this man chooses to submit his will and his life to God. His overriding desire is to please God, not himself. When faced with a tough decision, he will seek God and choose to do

what pleases his heavenly Father. In addition, he doesn't think he is always right and he doesn't always try to impose his will upon others. He is not driven by "self-will" but by "God's will."

"A lover of good." This trait speaks of the heart. The Bible teaches us to abstain from evil and stay away from those things that compromise us. However, it is possible for a Christian to sit on the fence of compromise and take part in things that are improper for a child of God. A church leader should not compromise by being involved with what is wrong or unscriptural. He cannot love evil or even flirt with it. He "loves what is good." This also implies he stands against evil.

"Holding fast the faithful word as he has been taught, that he may be able, by sound doctrine, both to exhort and convict those who contradict." This man believes God's Word and does not waver from biblical truth. Just as he is able to teach, he is also ready to exhort and convict those in the church who contradict God's Word. He will do it with conviction and to protect the Church, but he will also do it in love.

Overall Character

It is interesting that in listing the qualifications for a church leader Paul does not mention administrative skills, special training, or prior leadership positions. And, the qualified leader's resume is not necessarily filled with great deeds. Rather, he deals with character and relationship with God. Please understand: I am not saying that good leadership skills are not needed in the church. They are. But leadership skills can be learned. To God, a man's character and heart are the most important qualifications. The fact that a man has these qualities shows he has pursued God and wants to honor Him. He can be trusted to lead and maintain a high standard. However, if any leader does not have the right character, his leadership will falter, and others will be hurt.

But, you may ask, what about those who do not have these qualities and yet have great success? It's true that many people are successful in business, politics, or other fields without these character qualities. However, God's man cannot live that way. God has a standard for those who follow Him that is different than the world's standards.

We may emulate the world for a time, but if we are a true believer in Christ, God will work in our lives to bring us into His will and ways. He is committed to do that; we are His children. Remember, He is committed to conform us to the image (character) of Christ. Even if He gives us monetary success or important positions, the most important thing in our life is serving Him and wanting to please Him in all we do.

QUESTIONS FOR REFLECTION AND DISCUSSION

1. Do you find yourself eager about trying to please God in all areas of your life? Or, do you sense a conflict in yourself about trying to live a Christian life in all aspects of your life, including your work? Perhaps it's a bit of both. Describe how you navigate that tension and any areas of struggle below.

_____

_____

_____

_____

2. What do you think the reasons are for your struggle in the area(s) mentioned above? Is it fear of others' opinions? Are there habits or life patterns that need to be changed? God wants to help you. Below, write out a prayer asking Him to bring His help and resources into your life.

_____
_____
_____
_____

3. Whom do you know who might be able to mentor you, coach you, or pray for you in one or more of these areas?

_____
_____
_____
_____

TAKE A KNEE

Let's pray. *"Dear Father, I want to live for You 24/7. Please show me how. Give me the wisdom to live out the Christian life in all of my activities. I realize this does not mean I will not enjoy my life. Rather, I will do things with a right attitude and with the power of the Holy Spirit and not out of fear. Fill me, empower me, lead me, and give me Your insights."*

Chapter 5

Leadership in Action

Leading does not require a high-powered or charismatic personality. Too often, we equate leadership with personality. All types of personalities have become effective leaders. Some are very outgoing, some are quiet and reflective, some are more dominant and forceful, and others are humble and thoughtful. Being a good leader is something we learn by doing. Good training and mentoring are a great help. However, praying over your responsibilities and decisions, seeking godly wisdom, and studying God's Word are also essential for the Christian leader to learn and grow. We are going to discuss leadership style and then some essential aspects of what a leader does.

Guiding versus Driving

Before we get into practical ways to lead, we need to discuss our style or method of leadership. Let's consider an example.

Suppose you were a chariot driver with two well-trained horses. In fact, they were so well trained that all you had to do was to speak to them and they would to the rest. You would say, "Go!" and they would go. You would say "Fast!" and they would gallop. You would say, "Right," or, "Left," and they would turn, and so forth. All you had to do was give the needed instruction and they would get you there. These were great horses: fast, well trained, and requiring little effort on your part to get where you were going.

Now suppose your chariot and horses were loaned out to a friend. All of a sudden, you saw him go by and he was screaming at the horses, whipping them, using a lot of force on the reins, and causing the horses pain, to get the results he felt he needed. You are taken back and begin to try to get your friend's attention, to stop, so you could explain to him he was going about it all wrong. These horses do not need that type of driving. They just need to be guided and instructed. The "driver" is also taken back. All he has ever known is to drive the horses the way he does. After all, they are horses and need this type of leadership from the driver. This is the way you do it. Right?

While these may seem like extreme examples, they represent two types of leadership. One is a "team leader." He is a more collaborative type that looks to his employees as fellow workers. He/she teaches, explains, and guides workers, and sees them as a team to accomplish their task or to get the company where it needs to go. Together they get the job done.

Cooperatively, the leader works to get his part done and they all do theirs. They have team meetings where they discuss the things that need to be done, as well as the problems or obstacles. They discuss the obstacles they are encountering, or will encounter, and come up with a game plan to move forward. Assignments are given and everyone does their part. They hold update meetings, check on progress, make any adjustments, and continue to move forward. The leader and the team hold the members accountable. It is a team approach with the leader guiding the team.

The driver is more autocratic. He makes all of the decisions, makes all of the assignments, holds everyone accountable, and is not always kind in his approach. He may be given to anger when his expectations are not met, and there is fear among those working for him that he will get angry with them if they do not live up to his expectations. He uses intimidation, money (or fear of losing their job, thus no money), and forceful leadership to get things done his way. He is a "driver" and uses the whip, so to speak, to get the horses to do what he wants, when he wants.

Most leaders fall somewhere between these two approaches. The healthiest approach, which will get the best workers and results, is the collaborative or team leader approach. If you have to "whip" your workers to get the job done, then either you have the wrong worker or your approach has not allowed your workers to develop into the people they can be and you need them to be. Give them responsibility, let them work, and coach and lead them, and see if they can get the job done. Let them develop into the people they are capable of being. With that said, if they cannot get the job done, then they should be replaced. We'll discuss this more later.

I fully realize that the learning curve takes time and effort. Often, you need someone to step in who can get the job done right away. They need the skills and work ethic required and they need to perform right away. With that said, using the driver approach will not cause them to reach the potential in their job and, in the long run, the efforts you want to see. No one likes working for a bully or someone given to anger when a mistake is made. Good people will go elsewhere.

Developing a great team takes some time and effort. But if you have the right people, the leader will have much less stress, far more satisfaction, and the results will be greater.

In the family, a father needs to invest time into his children, teaching them character qualities and just enjoying them. If a father does not invest in his children when they are young, he may be spending a lot of time when they are teenagers trying to fix things. A father needs to ask himself why he is teaching and training his children. Is it because he wants to be proud of them so he can show them off and take the credit for any outstanding results, and make sure they do not soil his reputation? Or does he want them to reach their potential in life by becoming the people they can be, and to build scriptural truth into their lives. Love, patience, and consistency are important in a man's leadership when he is raising his children.

Lead Yourself and the Task

In leading others, a leader will need to gather information, make decisions, and establish direction for those he is leading. Obviously, a leader cannot establish direction and lead others unless he has direction himself. If you are still establishing direction and have others helping you, then have team meetings, gather information, give assignments, and guide the process.

If you don't have others to lead, you can establish direction for your life and how you will make decisions. You can establish disciplines in your life of seeking God and wanting to please Him. You can determine to guard your heart and your thought life and surrender your thoughts to God (Proverbs 4:23; Romans 12:2).

Gather needed information.

When Nehemiah got to Jerusalem, one of the first things he did was to go out and look at the task that had to be accomplished. He had to look over the situation and determine what needed to be done to get the job done. I can imagine as he looked over the task and the large amount of work that had to be done, that he prayed over Jerusalem, which was his workplace, and asked God for wisdom and understanding for how to accomplish this great task.

After he surveyed the work, he formulated a plan to accomplish it. He knew he needed to get others involved. He needed their help. He knew he needed the favor of God to get this done. He needed people to help him who had a desire to do so and put forth the effort required. They had to "buy into the plan" and be willing to follow him. He had to share his vision and goals and get them on board. Because God was leading Nehemiah, he was able to move the hearts of those who were to be part of the job, to get involved and work hard to get it done. God gave Nehemiah favor with those who were needed to get the job done.

A good leader gathers the best information he can. This includes research, wise counsel, and prayer—asking God for His help and direction. Gathering information to make a decision may be as simple as researching web sites of various products to make a good purchasing decision. Or it could be a complex process requiring extensive research in order to make strategic decisions involving many people and large amounts of money.

Regardless, a good leader tries to get practical information to make informed decisions. This is wisdom. Acting in haste and not doing your homework can lead to failure.

BEING A LEADER

> *"For which of you, intending to build a tower, does not sit down first and count the cost, whether he has enough to finish it—lest, after he has laid the foundation, and is not able to finish it, all who see it begin to mock him saying, 'This man began to build and was not able to finish.' Or what king, going to make war against another king, does not sit down first and consider whether he is able with ten thousand to meet him who comes against him with twenty thousand?"* (Luke 14:28-32)

Be organized and make a plan to get things done.

Nehemiah said to the people of Jerusalem, *"You see the trouble we are in. Jerusalem lies in ruins, and its gates have been burned with fire. Come, let us rebuild the wall of Jerusalem, and we will no longer be in disgrace. I also told them about the gracious hand of my God upon me and what the king had said to me. They replied, 'Let us start rebuilding.' So they began this good work."* (Nehemiah 2:17-18).

To get things done, a simple to-do list is still hard to beat, both on a daily basis and on a project level. Many people are well intentioned, but working strictly by memory just doesn't work. Not only can we forget to do the things that are important, we also may not get tasks done when needed—much to our dismay. I have supervised many people, and those who are organized and make daily lists are the ones who get things done. I'm the same. When I make and prioritize a daily list of the things I need to accomplish, I tend to get them done.

Nehemiah communicated the job to be done and got the people on board to begin the work. He developed the plan and then organized the people. He broke up the job into parts and assigned each part to a group to get it done.

When some leaders from other cities threatened to stop the work by force, he armed the workers and let those who threatened them know that they were armed and would fight if necessary. Here he showed courage and steadfastness.

When some under his leadership tried to discourage him he took a stand and let them know he would not be persuaded to stop the work but would complete the task. He showed great strength, determination, and leadership. He believed his task was of God and he was on a mission to complete it.

If you lead an organization, especially a large one, it is critical to prioritize what needs to get done and to plan on a larger scale. Determine the resources needed, both people and material, and come up with a plan to make it happen. Then involve others, get their counsel, and input. Bathe this process in prayer and ask for God's wisdom and leadership.

I have a friend who is president of an operating division of a national enterprise. His division is doing well. I asked him how he keeps things on track. He told me he has a daily meeting, each morning, with all of his department heads. They go over anything that has come up in the last day and what is needed to either solve the problem, keep them on track, or take advantage of any new opportunities.

Some mornings the meeting lasts 15 minutes. Other mornings the meeting will go until the issue is resolved and there is an action plan. In this way they keep the division on track to accomplish their goals and to resolve any issues needing to be resolved. Personally, he prays over his position and asks God for wisdom for him to lead his company.

Not all leaders have daily meetings with their team. Some meet weekly. Some have weekly meetings with individual team members and monthly all team meetings. The point is to communicate and keep the team together and moving forward.

As a Christian, it is important to remember that God wants to be involved in all areas of our life, business and personal. Seeking Him for wisdom regarding decisions is not only wise, but essential. Too often many Christian businessmen think that God is there when we are in a crisis, or when it involves "spiritual matters" such as church issues, missions or those in full time vocational ministry.

But involving God in all areas of life is both practical and spiritual. We are His servants and His priests. Our work and our lives are His concern and He wants us to involve Him in every part of our life. Nehemiah saw his work as given to him from God. *He believed his tasks were God-given.* We should also. Our God stands ready to help, lead, and guide us. His resources are unlimited.

When I was in my twenties, I worked for a company that developed large master-planned communities that were usually several thousand acres. It was a complex process that involved developing a plan for the property, getting local government approvals for their plans, dividing up the plan into different pieces or parts, and getting members of the team to take charge of them.

Each week they would meet and go over the project piece by piece and get an update from each person who was to get things done. They would hold each other accountable for their work and make decisions of what needed to be done the following week. By dividing up the work and putting people in charge of each part, then defining what needed to be done and working toward it, the project moved forward and things were accomplished until their work was completed. A large complex project was completed by the team. As I watched this take place, I learned a great deal about a team working together to accomplish a large task that none of them could accomplish on their own.

Many of you reading this may not have management roles and tasks like I have described. You may have a job and things to do at home. But at your job, your have responsibilities and things you are responsible for and at home you also have things to get done. You can make a list of the things you need to get done at work. You can also make list of the things you need to get done at home. Then you can set aside time to get these things done.

For example, let's say you are an electrician and working on homes or buildings each day, installing the wires, receptacles, switches, panels, and other items that are needed. You can be organized and make sure you have the right materials and tools before starting. You can organize the job to make the work orderly and efficient. You can keep the job site clean so there is not excess waste or injuries, and when others view your work they will know you take pride in what you do.

I realize some people are naturally organized and others seem to "wing it." But all of us can learn, through practice, to be as organized as we need to be and do our work well. By taking leadership of ourself and our work, we are developing leadership qualities.

Make good decisions.

Leadership means making decisions, whether large or small. Some decisions are easy. At other times, they can be very difficult because of what is at stake. Knowing when to make decisions and when to step back and wait for more information or guidance can be critical. Often, taking time to consider the decision, pray about it, and getting wise counsel, will bring the issues into focus, making the right decision clear.

We should not be in a hurry to make major decisions. If we do not have peace, we should not act (Philippians 4:7-8; Colossians

3:15). There are times God wants us to wait on Him for direction. If we get in a hurry, we can miss God and make the wrong decision. As we pray and seek God, read His Word, and get good counsel, we will become wiser and more able to make consistently good decisions.

Seek wise counsel.

No one has all of the answers. A good leader will seek wise counsel. This shows humility. Wise counsel can save you from great mistakes. Proverbs 1:5 says, *"A wise man will hear and increase learning. And a man of understanding will attain wise counsel."*

We should be willing to listen to those we are leading as well as getting counsel from outside sources—many times wise counsel will come from those under our leadership. I have found from experience that getting the appropriate people around a table and discussing direction, ideas, potential problems, and solutions to problems often brings out wisdom, practical insight, and direction. God will often speak through the team members. If no solution seems clear, then put it on hold, take time to pray, and wait until you have clearer direction.

Lead the People

Leadership is being and doing. Both of these come into play when we've done our planning and begin to include and lead others.

While the following practices are used often in the work world, there are practical ways to use these principles in the family, the church and any other situation we find ourselves in.

Good leadership is good leadership, regardless of where it is practiced.

Remember, our family is not a business. If we are rigid when dealing with family matters, there will be no joy. We should be loving and kind in all we do with our family. We can be a good leader, firm when needed, and loving and kind at the same time. We should extend grace and forgiveness to those we lead, as well as hold them accountable. Families should be places of love, fun, learning, and training. This can be accomplished in an informal manner that fosters a rich family life. I encourage you to keep the following aspects of being and doing in mind as you lead those God has entrusted to you.

Communicate decisions and direction.

As leaders, we need to give direction, or vision, to those working for us. A lack of communication can cause confusion and, in some cases, have dire consequences. Proverbs 29:18 says, *"Where there is no vision, the people are unrestrained"* (another translation says, *"they perish"*).

As leaders involve others in a project, they must communicate needed information and direction to each person or department. Decisions must be clearly communicated as well as the role each person or group must play to accomplish the goal.

In the home, the husband and wife work as a team to teach and communicate about behavior, attitudes, and family direction. Clear communication between the husband and wife, and with the children, is important to peace and harmony in the family. The husband and wife should develop a family culture that is positive and loving. Doing this will reap great benefits in the family.

You do not have to be a skilled orator to communicate well. You communicate needed information to those involved in your life or those under your leadership. Learning to communicate is not hard. In fact it's easy to get started. Just open your mouth and begin to communicate! If you're not very good at it, don't worry, you'll improve with practice.

Show the proper example.

Nehemiah was among the workers rebuilding the wall, encouraging them, overseeing the work and keeping the work going. When problems came up he responded by providing solutions and ways to keep progressing while addressing the problems.

A good leader leads not only by communicating but also by doing. People watch how we lead, how we get our part of the job done, and our attitudes. Part of doing is the example one sets. People watch our lives, and our actions can help lead others. Even if we are not in authority over others, many times we can have positive influence in others' lives by helping them.

I fully realize that some people are more gifted than others administratively. Some leaders need administratively gifted people around them to get things done. They may be visionaries who need others to carry out the visions. But a leader has things he needs to do. If he doesn't do his part, then there can be confusion, disappointment, frustration, and workers may choose to go elsewhere.

While different leader may choose "their work" differently than other leaders, whatever "their work" is, they should be faithful to get it done so the others on the team see they are committed and diligent. It's difficult to hold others accountable if we are not willing to be.

While we don't know all of Nehemiah's giftings or his skill set, we do know he stayed in the midst of the work, did his part, encouraged the other workers, and did not abandon the ship. He didn't just sit around sipping wine and barking out orders to the others. Whatever his part of the work was, he got it done.

Suggesting how to accomplish a task or even getting involved to get it done can show great initiative and mark us for leadership. Often just rolling up our sleeves and getting to work can show leadership. It gets the job started or keeps it going. When we take the lead to get the job done, others often will join in. Jesus led by example. His disciples learned both by what He said and what He did. His actions taught, His words taught, His life taught. So can ours.

Be available.

Nehemiah knew what was going on. He was there living with those he was leading and understood the problems and issues. He was determined to get the work completed because it was in everyone's best interest to do so.

It's tough to lead others effectively if you are not available to them. One leader told me, somewhat proudly, that he made himself available to those under his leadership every Monday from 9:00 a.m. till noon. I wondered, *What about the other 40 or 50 hours in the workweek?*

Unfortunately, problems don't always show up only between 9:00 and noon on Mondays. Things come up, new information is discovered, and decisions need to be made. If we have competent people under us, they may not need as much leadership from us. But if we are in charge, we need to be available to lead, answer questions, and give input and direction as needed.

What about in the family? What if a Dad said he was only available on Monday evenings and everyone had to figure it out the rest of the time? It would be difficult for Dad to hold his children accountable for bad decisions if he was unavailable for help, guidance, and counsel.

Follow up and hold people accountable.

After Nehemiah had rebuilt the wall and set the temple in order, he appointed those to lead and oversee the city, the temple and the people. He delegated responsibility and authority, and communicated clearly what needed to be done. He left those in charge of key areas whom he believed were able to get the job done properly. He made provision for the priests and set things in order. He then left for a period of time to return to the king, give a report, and resume his service. He understood that, though he was the governor, the leader of Jerusalem, he in turn was accountable to the king whom he served.

Though we might lead in our company, our church, or our family, we are accountable to those in authority over us. And we are always accountable to God for our actions and attitudes. We are His servants and He is very interested in how we lead. He realizes we will make mistakes, but He is interested in our hearts, our attitudes, and whether or not we are learning as we go.

Nehemiah returned to the king to give a report on his activities. After a time, Nehemiah asked the king for permission to return to Jerusalem and see how things were going. Once he got there, he found out many of the leaders were not carrying out their responsibilities as they were supposed to. He would not compromise the things that needed to be done as they were critically important and affected all.

Nehemiah quickly dealt with the situation and with the leaders who were being negligent. He reprimanded them and once again set things in order. In some cases, he disciplined those who had violated the standards that needed to be upheld and let them know that compromise in these areas could not be tolerated. He held them accountable (Nehemiah 13).

The leader is the captain of the ship and must keep it on course. Many leaders falter at this point; they do not like holding others accountable. Often those conversations can be difficult and even gut-wrenching. Yet, a good system of follow up is critical, especially when much is at stake.

In a family setting, follow up will most likely be very informal and may involve a few questions such as, *How are you doing on the project we discussed? How are you doing on your schoolwork and tests? Let's go over your homework and see how you did. Did you do the things we discussed?*

At times, a leader must deal with bad attitudes and actions. In the home, this must be done in a loving manner to correct and instruct for the sake of the offender and for the rest of the family. Children need to be held accountable for their sakes. If they aren't, your instructions will become meaningless.

Even when correction or discipline is necessary, your family needs to know that you care for them and that they are loved. You can show this by your attitude toward them, your actions, the time you invest with them, and the enjoyment you display when you spend time with them. Building them up verbally and telling them you love them will convey to them your love and how important they are to you.

In a company, holding people accountable and providing follow up may involve scheduled meetings or reports, weekly or daily, to give feedback and direction. People want to know how they are doing in their work. Holding people accountable requires effort and follow through. However, it keeps people from wandering off course and lets the leader know the type of people who work for him. Do they get their job done? Are they reliable? Do they do quality work? Are they open to constructive input or criticism?

Holding people accountable and micromanaging are not the same. Most, if not all people, do not enjoy someone brooding over them and watching their every move, ready to jump on them for any mistakes. This does not develop responsible employees who become great at their jobs and who can handle the job that needs to be done.

Delegating tasks, giving direction, allowing them to work independently, and then following up to make sure things are on course allows people to get the job done and show "their stuff." It also allows the "boss" to see how they handle things and if they are capable.

In the parable of the talents (Matthew chapter 25), the master gave the servants sums of money and the task to manage it wisely and increase it. He then left to attend to business in another country and after a period of time came back and asked for an accounting of how they did.

Most employees will need more supervision and follow up than giving a task and going away for possibly months or years and expecting them to work independently without any supervision. But the principle is to give responsibility, allow a person to work to accomplish the task, give input and supervision as needed, and hold them accountable. The servants who acted wisely and managed the money well were promoted, given more responsibility and praised for their results.

Regular follow up can show the leader who his stars are and who needs help. It will also show those who are unable or unwilling to get the job done and need to be replaced or moved to another position where they can be productive. Sometimes good people are in the wrong job. At other times we just have the wrong person.

Take action with those who undermine efforts.

One task of a leader is to determine if those responsible to get things done are competent to do so. If not, for their sake and the sake of the organization, they must be reassigned or replaced. This can be crucial. An unwillingness to take action may cause big problems and even failure. One person who is wrongly placed or who undermines our efforts can have a negative impact on many.

I am not talking about honest disagreement. That can be healthy at times. I am talking about those who have a critical attitude, are rebellious, untrustworthy, or just incapable of doing their work at the level that is needed.

Most people can be turned around with some effort and coaching, or moved to a job that is a better fit. However, with others, the best thing is to let them go. An effective leader recognizes this. Not dealing with the issue is unfair to them, those they work with, and to you. A good leader has to learn not to avoid tough situations. He must show courage and do what is needed.

James was a good leader with above average results. He organized his team and clearly communicated direction; his efforts were paying off. However, he had a weakness: at times he would be too tolerant with those who were longtime employees. He allowed people to stay in jobs that had outgrown them. His desire to "go the extra mile" with them and to be loyal to them began to cause departments to falter as some of the department heads failed to give effective leadership.

As he tried to turn around those who were faltering, he determined to work closer with them by having weekly meetings to coach and counsel them. Some of those in the organization began to share with him the problems that were occurring and causing morale to drop in the organization.

Eventually, as he began to hold those accountable who were faltering, they turned on him and behind his back began to be critical of him with those in their departments. Their critical attitudes spread through the organization. When he finally let them go, the atmosphere changed. Even so, there was some fallout. Additional employees had been affected by the critical attitudes and had to be let go. James learned that keeping people in a job they could not perform well affected the entire organization. And the fallout took time to repair. Had he acted earlier many of the problems he now had to "fix" could have been avoided.

It is easy to confuse our responsibility to love and care for others with our responsibility to lead, be a good steward, and hold those accountable under our leadership. Allowing people to do poor work, not be faithful, waste time and resources, undermine you, undermine your efforts, lead others astray, and doing nothing about it is not being a good leader—nor is it doing what is best for the individual.

Doing what is best for them is instructing them, coaching them, encouraging them, and if their behavior is negative and affecting others, correcting them for their own good and the good of all affected. They must learn what is right and appropriate, and if they are under your leadership it is your responsibility to set the standard and uphold it.

Have a good attitude and encourage others.

Nobody wants to be under the leadership of someone who is sour and critical, or heavy-handed. Being positive and cheerful will affect your family, your business, and everyone you meet. We all need to be encouraged and praised. Even when it's necessary to correct others and point out problem areas, we can do it in such a way as to encourage them to do what is right.

The Bible tells church leaders not to "lord it (their leadership) over others" (see 1 Peter 5:1-3). This refers to our attitude and how we exercise our authority. A prideful person will lead in a way to build himself up and promote himself. His or her attitude is that others are there just to serve them and accomplish their goals. However, the Bible warns against pride and says it will lead to our eventual destruction (Proverbs 16:18). If we are prideful, heavy-handed, and trying to promote ourselves, we are using our leadership position to promote our agenda without considering what is best for those we are leading.

Many feel that as a leader they need to try to be perfect, or project that they are. Guess what. None of us are perfect. People will see who you are and you cannot hide it. Trying to be perfect just doesn't work.

Rather, realize you are an imperfect person and are always needing to grow and improve. You try to do what is right and lead others not because you are the perfect example, but because you have been given that responsibility. Others can see your humanity and still respect you as they learn that your motives are good and you are committed to lead and do the best job you can. You'll never be perfect, but you can be a great leader.

Be fair and just.

Great leaders exude a sense of fairness and honesty; they are just, fair, and do what is right. Not only does this help to promote positive morale in the company (or family or ministry), but it also encourages those around us to act in a just and fair manner. Fair and just leaders create a sense of security for those under their authority; they know if they do their work to the best of their ability, their leader will recognize that and they will be rewarded.

Promote the growth of those under our leadership.

Whether in our family, ministry, or business sphere, we want those around us to grow as individuals. They should develop their skills, grow in character, and lead fruitful and productive lives. We should look for ways to encourage those under our leadership in these areas. Those who go the extra mile should be acknowledged and rewarded for their efforts. In the parable of the talents (Matthew 25:14-28), the master praised those who did a good job. He rewarded them, promoted them, and let them know they were valued. Everyone needs praise and positive confirmation when they are doing things right and getting the job done, especially if they are doing it well. If you don't take care of a good employee, he or she may go elsewhere.

Take a stand for what is right.

Great leaders live by principle. Godly leaders live by godly principles. Great leaders know when to be flexible and when to stand firm based on the principles of God's Word. Some of those principles would be truthfulness, acting in honesty and integrity, doing what is best for all, and trying to please God in all we do. For a great example of this, read Acts 4.

Pray.

A godly leader prays over his work, his decisions, his direction, and asks God for His leadership. He prays for wisdom, insight, discernment, and understanding. Look at Acts 13:1-4, 2 Chronicles 20:1-30, and 2 Samuel 5:17-25. In all of these passages, God gave wisdom and direction when His people sought Him and prayed. Take time to seek God daily through prayer and Bible reading, and pray over your work, your family, your employees, and all areas of your life.

Stay the Course

No matter where we lead, it is important that we get the job done. Helping your family or your company to stay the course can determine whether a leader is mediocre or excellent. Many get started and get things going and then falter along the way. They may get sidetracked, allow themselves to lose interest, or lose their priorities.

Remember, especially when others are involved, you have a responsibility to get the job done. Keep yourself in the game. Don't allow your interest to wane. Pray for God's help and guard your heart and desires.

When you are in charge, others are watching your example. This is part of your ministry. Your work, your attitudes, and your leadership all speak of who you are and have impact on others. Your ministry is living your life in a manner that speaks to others the message that God desires to speak through you.

Some people are visionaries and not gifted administratively. They have a vision for the project or goal but need others to carry it out. This can be accomplished by getting the right team in place. However, the leader needs to stay in place to keep the team moving in the right direction.

We have covered a lot of ground in this section. Let's summarize some of the points we discussed above concerning leadership.

1. Determine the task and the direction for what needs to be done.
2. Gather the information that is needed. Do your "due diligence."
3. Come up with a plan.

4. Pray over your tasks and goals and get wise counsel. Make the best decisions you can.
5. Communicate with those helping you. Communicate vision, the tasks that need to be done, and who is to do what. Get input from the team and communicate your decisions to them. Give regular updates along the way to to those who need it to keep them informed.
6. Hold those under your leadership accountable. Remember to encourage and give praise to those who are working hard at getting the job done and getting good results. Take action to either replace or re-direct those who are undermining or hindering the progress of the work. Don't be afraid to replace and let go those that are being negative or hindering the work if that is what is needed.
7. As a leader, keep a good attitude toward the tasks that need to be done and toward the team. Keep the morale positive and upbeat. Encourage those working with you.
8. Always be fair and act with integrity in all you do.
9. Stand for what is right and promote work ethics that are based on treating others fairly and just.
10. Pray over all you do and ask God to give you wisdom, insight and His guidance in all of your activities. Seek His wisdom and ask Him to lead you.

QUESTIONS FOR REFLECTION AND DISCUSSION

1. As you read the list above, where did you sense God saying, "Well done," to you?

2. Were there any areas in which you sense He wishes you to grow?

3. What are one or two steps you could take to begin to take more initiative in this area?

TAKE A KNEE

Let's pray: *"Father, help me in these areas of leadership. Help me to practice the skills and habits I need in order to be more effective in my responsibilities. I don't desire to be rigid and inflexible, or passive and disorganized—but rather to be productive and faithful, and accomplish all You desire me to. Help me to grow and develop into the leader I need to be. I commit this to You."*

Chapter 6

START WHERE YOU ARE

I got married when I was twenty, and we started a family right away. I dropped out of college in my junior year and took a job to support my family. I kept going back to school part time, hoping to finish. I went to four different universities! However, as time passed, I had to repeat some of my classes as the school would no longer honor some of my class credits because so much time had passed.

Finally, I decided to finish. I realized that if I focused and spent the time studying that I spent watching television or doing unnecessary things, I could get it done. At the time, I was in a senior management position, and I could not neglect my work.

My wife had to buy into my decision and subsequent effort; she was a great support. I had to make a plan and be disciplined for two years, but I completed my degree with honors. The key to finishing was taking leadership of myself, creating a plan, using my time wisely, and staying the course.

You may be in a different place than I was; we all have our own set of circumstances. But we all start in the same place: where we are *right now*. At some point, we simply take the first steps. As I found with my university experience, we can accomplish far more than we realize when we come up with a plan and take the steps to execute it.

Simple Steps to Action

Planning does not mean you become rigid, but we do need to be disciplined and diligent. Developing some simple habits regarding the use of your time can help you to be far more productive and achieve your goals. This may be difficult at first for those who like to wing it. Nevertheless, everyone can learn to be more organized or use their time more effectively. (If you are a father, cultivating these simple skills and teaching them to your children will pay big dividends.) We've already touched on these throughout the study, but here is a simple summary:

a. Think through the tasks or projects that you need or desire to do. Write them down.
b. Think through the steps necessary to get them done. Decide on the resources needed to get them done. List the steps and resources.
c. Make a daily to-do list from your steps, so that you begin to work on your plan daily.
d. At the end of each day, take a few minutes to look over your "to-do list" and think through the next day. List the things you need to accomplish tomorrow. This will cause you to be more productive. Then each morning review your list again and begin.

To some this may sound rigid. Others love lists and love making them and getting the tasks on the list done. Not all things need to be organized in this way. Some are straightforward and you just do them. But making a simple list of what you need to get done is a great benefit both to you and to those around you.

With that said, life can be messy and is not always neatly organized. We also want to be flexible. Some tasks may take longer than we originally thought. Some jobs grow into much larger projects than we thought. Things come up that aren't on your list but need to be dealt with. I have had days when my list was untouched at the end of the day. That's okay; simply begin again the next day.

"But What if I'm Not Qualified?"

We can feel that we simply are not qualified to lead—particularly after looking at the task that needs to be done. The good news is that we do not have to feel we are ready in order to answer God's call. I like the saying, "God does not always call the well equipped, but He does equip the called." If God is leading you to do something, He will equip (train, give wisdom, give solutions to problems), along the way.

God's calling is not always to the qualified, but He qualifies the called.

One of the more detailed discourses in the Bible is the one between God and Moses in Exodus 3–4. Few dialogues in the Bible cover two chapters, especially between God and a man.

Moses' calling was very important; it was a central part of God fulfilling His promises to Abraham and the nation of Israel. Even though God used a burning bush to appear to Moses and spoke to him directly, Moses was reluctant to respond. He did not think he was qualified to lead the Israelites out of captivity and into the land God had promised.

> *But Moses said to God, "Who am I that I should go to Pharaoh, and that I should bring the children of Israel out of Egypt?"*
>
> *So He said, "I will certainly be with you. And this shall be a sign to you that I have sent you: when you have brought the people out of Egypt, you shall serve God on this mountain."*
>
> *Then Moses said to God, "Indeed, when I come to the children of Israel and say to them, 'The God of your fathers has sent me to you,' and they say to me, 'What is His name?' What shall I say to them?"*
>
> *And God said to Moses, "I AM WHO I AM." Thus you shall say to the children of Israel, "I AM has sent me to you."*
> (Exodus 3:11-14)

The discussion did not stop there. Moses gave excuse after excuse. He told God that surely someone else could do this. Moses simply did not want the job. God finally actually got angry with Moses for his resistance and unbelief. It wasn't that Moses was just doubting himself; he was doubting that God would be with him and give him what was needed to get the job done. He just wasn't trusting God to be faithful. He was saying to God, " How do I know I will be successful in getting this done? How do I know You will come through for me when I need You?"

Focusing on himself, Moses may have resisted for any number of reasons. A good thing to keep in mind is that Moses was not part of a local church where the Bible was taught every week. In fact, there were no churches and there was no Bible; it hadn't been written yet. He had been a shepherd in the desert for 40 years and had made a life for himself there. Now God appears in a burning bush and says,"Let's change everything. Leave your life behind as you know it and go back to Egypt. I will miraculously work through you to make Pharaoh let the Israelites go."

Remember, Moses developed a desire to help the nation of Israel when they were slaves to Egypt and he was brought up as a part of Pharaoh's household (see Exodus 2). He killed an Egyptian soldier who was abusing an Israelite. He was exposed for this and had to flee for his life. He then spent 40 years as a shepherd. He tried to do a good thing in the wrong way at the wrong time and it failed, something he never forgot. Now he was being asked to do the same thing he desired to do forty years earlier when he failed.

What plagued Moses? Was it the fear of Pharaoh's army and power? Was it that he had previously tried and failed? Did he feel inadequate? Was he ashamed of his past actions? Perhaps, because so much time had passed, he had given up on ever being able to fulfill the desire in his heart. Possibly, he had come to feel inadequate. Whatever his feelings, they surfaced when God appeared and called him to the task. His destiny was in the balance. He tried to back out. He insisted that he wasn't the man for the job. But he did obey and God used him greatly.

Another example of someone feeling unsure and inadequate about his calling was Israel's first king, Saul. In 1 Samuel 10, we have the account of Samuel the prophet calling Israel together to anoint Saul as king. According to custom, they drew lots, and the lot fell to Saul's household, and then to Saul. This was a miraculous happening.

Samuel had previously told Saul that God had chosen him to be Israel's first king, anointed him with oil, and spoke prophetic sayings over him that came true. The fact that he then was chosen by casting random lots over millions of people should have been enough confirmation. However, when the people who had been casting lots searched for him, they found him hiding among the baggage. He felt inadequate. Maybe he felt his heritage or family was not prominent enough to merit such a position. Perhaps he was unsure of his leadership abilities or his courage for such a task.

God calls whom He wills to serve and lead. Many people God calls feel inadequate to accomplish the task. That is because they are. Over time, God trains and equips, grants wisdom and insight, and the called one grows into the task. The most important thing is God's calling. Whom He calls, He anoints or equips.

This means that His Spirit is present and works in and through the person to carry out the task. God wants us to fulfill our calling in spite of our shortcomings. It drives us to our knees (a good place to be) and makes us realize our need for God to help us. Being dependent on Him is exactly where He wants us to be.

Whether one is called, like Moses or Saul, to positions of prominence, or one is called to responsibility in everyday tasks, God will supply the resources, wisdom, and insight to get the job done.

We should work as though the outcome is up to us, but pray and seek God knowing the final outcome is up to Him.

Lean on God

There are basic things all leaders should do. First, we must take leadership of ourselves. We should learn to use our time wisely, be responsible, take initiative, and get things done. It is critical to understand that doing things in a manner that is pleasing to God, and in keeping with His Word, are the foundations to Christian life, and Christian leadership.

- If you are single, you are called to take charge of yourself and move ahead as God directs. Develop the disciplines you need for your life by practicing them.
- If you are married, you are called to be a responsible husband and encourage your wife to join you in seeking God and His direction for your lives.
- If you are a father, you are called to lead your family.
- If you have those under your authority or leadership at work or any other arena, you are called to lead them in a manner honoring to God.

Nevertheless, there is not just one way to be a good leader. There are many styles of leadership. Often we get caught up in trying to be like others. However, God knows our personality, our talents and gifts, His purpose for us, and what we are best suited to do. We should not try to be another person, but rather seek God and ask Him to make us the person He wants us to be. Allow Him to mold the clay of our heart and character. His work is sure. He knows what He is doing! To some this may sound rigid. Others love lists and love making them and getting the things on the list done.

In the Bible, was David like Samuel, or Daniel like Jeremiah? Was the apostle Peter like the apostle John? These men had much different personalities and gifts. But as they yielded to God and sought Him, making Him the chief prize, God molded them and used them beyond their natural abilities.

Because of different personalities, talents, aptitudes, and giftings, people will do things in different ways in order to get things done. While some may initially shrink back and are unsure, others jump with enthusiasm into the task they believe God has given them. In either case, looking to God to empower and lead you for the task is where your focus should be. Your part is to seek Him for wisdom, apply yourself to your tasks, and do your best.

By the way, there will be problems, surprises, and maybe some roadblocks along the way. Theses are so God can show you He is with you as you seek Him and He shows up and things get worked out, sometimes miraculously!

God is the one who gives us wisdom, blesses our work, and helps us succeed in it. He will give us understanding in our areas of responsibility. He wants to do that. However, He wants us to seek Him regarding our work and ask for His help. He delights to give us the insight we need as we seek Him for it. God knew when He called Moses that Moses could not accomplish the task without His divine help. God was prepared to give it. He had a plan Moses didn't know about at the time. First Moses had to surrender to God, and then God's plan unfolded a step at a time.

> *"Trust in the Lord with all your heart, and lean not on your own understanding; in all your ways acknowledge Him, and He shall direct your paths. Do not be wise in your own eyes, fear the Lord and depart from evil, it will be health to your flesh, and strength to your bones. Honor the Lord with your possessions and with the first fruits of all your increase; so your barns will be filled with plenty, and your vats will overflow with new wine. My son, do not despise the chastening (training) of the Lord, nor detest His correction; for whom the Lord loves He corrects, just as a father the son in whom he delights"* (Proverbs 3:3-12, see also verses 13-18).

Remember this verse also: *"I can do all things through Christ who strengthens me"* (Philippians 4:13, NKJV). God will equip you for your tasks. He is faithful.

QUESTIONS FOR REFLECTION AND DISCUSSION

1. Do you ever, like Moses, feel unqualified to respond to God's call on your life? Why or why not?

2. Finding God's will for our life requires surrender and obedience. In what ways do You sense Him asking you surrender to Him as He shows you His will for your life? Are you willing? If not, what holds you back?

3. God gives all His children talents, abilities, and spiritual gifts. What would you say yours are? (You may want to ask some people close to you to tell you what they see in you.)

4. How and where has God uniquely wired and placed you to lead? (Think of your family, your work, your church, or other areas of your life.)

_____

_____

_____

_____

TAKE A KNEE

Let's pray: *"Father, I acknowledge before You that I have shortcomings and weaknesses. I am human and sometimes feel like I fail. However, I believe You will always be with me and help me. I want to be the leader You want me to be in the areas You give me to lead. I also realize how important it is to take charge of myself and develop good disciplines and seek You to build the character You desire in my life. As I seek You, show me the things You desire to do in my life. Show me how to be the leader You desire me to be."*

Chapter 7

BEING A LEADER IS NOT ALWAYS EASY

When Nehemiah began to rebuild the wall, he immediately encountered resistance and those who tried to stop his work. *"But when Sanballat the Horonite, Tobiah the Ammonite official and Gershem the Arab heard about it, they mocked and ridiculed us, 'What is this you are doing?' They asked. 'Are you rebelling against the king?'"* (Nehemiah 2:19)

Again and again his enemies tried to stop the work and discourage him. At one point, they recruited some of his own people to discourage him and try to make him stop out of fear. They told him his enemies were going to attack him and force him to stop if he did not stop willingly. They told Nehemiah, *"Wherever you turn, they will attack you"* (Nehemiah 4:12).

Nehemiah's response was, *"Therefore I stationed some of the people behind the lowest points of the wall at the exposed places, posting them by families, with their swords, spears and bows. After I looked things over, I stood up and said to the nobles, the officials and the rest of the people, 'Don't be afraid of them. Remember the Lord, who is great and awesome, and fight for your brothers, your sons and your daughters, your wives and your homes'". When our enemies heard that we were aware of their plot and that God had frustrated it, we all returned to the wall, each to his own work.* (Please also read Nehemiah 4:13-23.)

Most good efforts encounter opposition or problems along the way. A leader cannot crumble when opposition comes. He should seek God and get good counsel, if needed, to get the proper perspective to move things forward.

Sometimes opposition brings up things we need to consider and make a part of our plans. At other times, it is just opposition fashioned by the enemy to stop us. God will give us wisdom how to proceed. In Nehemiah's case, this opposition was designed to stop him from doing what God had called him to do. Nehemiah knew he needed to move forward and did so. He did not let the opposition stop him.

Nehemiah had to deal with his enemies from without, those who opposed him from within, and to keep encouraging and keep on task those who had to get the work done. He had to deal with difficult circumstances almost from the beginning, and throughout the 55 days it took to rebuild the wall. The fact he did it in 55 days was amazing. It could easily have taken a year or more.

After the initial job was done of rebuilding the wall, he then led the people to seek the Lord and put Him first in their lives. He had to oversee the leaders under him and deal with disloyalty, rebellion, and apathy. Since Nehemiah was human, he had to deal with a wide range of emotions: disappointment, the temptation to give into fear, the temptation to quit or get sidetracked, feeling betrayed, those under his leadership being disloyal, and the temptation to get discouraged.

But he was quite determined and would not quit. He was a man who sought God and believed God was there to help him. Above all he trusted God and believed God would help him in his tasks. He encouraged himself in the Lord.

What does it mean to "encourage yourself in the Lord"? It means when we are down or discouraged, we remind ourself that God is with us. He said, "I will never desert you nor will I ever forsake you" (Hebrews 13:5). As we remind ourself of that and that God is faithful, we encourage ourself in the Lord.

Remember the story of David in chapter 1 and how he had to encourage himself in the Lord? At times, we must do this. This incident was a real test of David's leadership. And it came just before his greatest triumph at that point in his life. He could have given up, fled to escape from his men, and drowned in discouragement. But he "strengthened himself in the Lord." He told himself the Lord was with him and would not let him down. There was a solution to this mess. David turned to God and believed He would help him.

Even if you like to lead, there are times that are challenging and even tough. If you're called to the task, God will help you. But that doesn't mean you may not be tempted to throw in the towel occasionally. Developing a great team and spending time with them can provide some great camaraderie. Seeing goals get accomplished and tasks completed can bring a sense of satisfaction and victory.

But along the way there are always challenges; it goes with the territory. The bigger the goal, the greater the challenges. But we serve a big God; one who is bigger than any challenge we may face.

Anything God leads us to do, we can accomplish. We may hit hard spots and challenges, but as we seek Him who has all knowledge and wisdom, He will help us. As I have said, often He is waiting for us to call on Him so He can show Himself to be strong on our behalf. He has promised, *"I will never leave you or forsake you"* (Matthew 13:5).

Carrying the responsibility of leadership may at times seem overwhelming. At times we may feel like we can't (or maybe don't want to anymore), get the job done. Realizing our inadequacy and humanity does not mean we can't accomplish our task. Often realizing our need and going to God is just what He wanted. He wants to show Himself faithful to us and to His word. He wants to act on our behalf.

As we lead, we will grow. Our abilities will increase and our perspective will change. And, as we learn to trust God more, the peace in our life will increase. We won't get rattled or discouraged as easily and we will have greater confidence, confidence that God is always there to help us. We will become more steadfast and determined. But let's talk about some of the things we may experience along the way.

Tough Decisions

A leader will face tough decisions. It may be letting someone go whom you like or value. It may be admitting you were wrong about a major decision. It may be dealing with tough opposition. It may be facing unforeseen difficulty. It may be running short of money or needing more than you thought (which happens a lot). Whatever the problem, it comes as no surprise to God. He saw it coming way before you did.

I have found that as I pray and ask God to help me in all I do, He does just that. There have been many times I have tried to force my way forward, only to face bigger challenges. When I have stopped and called out to God and asked for His wisdom and help, He always supplies it. I have gotten myself in messes due to my willfulness and thinking I always knew what to do. I have seen God work in my life as I have humbled myself and admitted I needed His help and asked Him to get involved in my circumstances.

In 2006, the real estate market fell apart. As a homebuilder, I was faced with multi-million dollar loans and obligations and nothing was working out. I really wasn't sure what to do. I could not control the economy, the government, or the housing industry. I would wake up in the middle of the night wondering what would happen.

In prayer one day, the Lord posed a question to me: "Do you really trust me?' I knew what He was asking me and what it meant. Did I really trust Him to help me in these circumstances? If so, I could relax and watch Him work. During the process, two lawsuits were filed against me by lenders. The lenders had actually defaulted in their loans with me, but they were pursuing me for money, much more than I had. I realized I could live my life in fear, worry, and doubt or I could choose to trust God. I knew I had done nothing wrong and was trying to work things out honorably.

My attorney suggested I consider bankruptcy to discharge the lawsuits. But, after prayer, I believed God would somehow work all things out. My wife and I prayed for a number of months and continued to trust God. Eventually, one lender took me to arbitration and I won. The other, who had also caused the problem themselves, settled for pennies on the dollar and I was able to pay it. In a short period, I saw potentially millions of dollars of obligations go away completely, and my credit and good standing were intact.

Interestingly, when the economy began to strengthen, one of those lenders approached me and wanted to do business with me again. He recognized I had not caused the problem and that I had acted in good faith. I had to make some tough decisions and trust God to help me through this difficult time. During the process, God worked in my life and made some changes in me, my attitudes and thinking, and in my heart. He was faithful.

There was another time I had several employees that were causing problems. I liked them personally, but realized that if they did not go, it would affect the entire organization. These were department heads and their attitudes were affecting the organization. I realized something had to be done but struggled with the alternatives.

It is not easy firing people, especially those you like. It takes courage and trust in God to supply another person you need after you let one go. I have always looked at it as an opportunity to upgrade. I have always believed God would supply someone better if I needed to let someone go. But at times I have struggled doing what needed to be done. I have found that I have a faithful God. He truly is a friend who sticks closer than a brother, as the Bible says. He supplies what I need. As I lean on Him, my burden is lifted and made light. As I trust in Him, I see Him work in my life.

I am still learning, but I have experienced God working in greater ways in my life and my trust in Him and my joy in serving Him is growing. Take a plunge! Let Him lead you and take on the things He wants to accomplish through you. Don't be afraid to tackle the big things. You serve a big God!

QUESTIONS FOR REFLECTION AND DISCUSSION

1. After this study, how would you now define leadership?

2. If you feel inadequate to lead, how have you gained courage to get started?

3. How would you describe the effect you want your leadership to have in your home?

   In your workplace?

4. What are three key thoughts or practices you want to take away from this study?

- _____

- _____

- _____

TAKE A KNEE

Lets pray: *"Father, You know what You have called to be and what You want me to accomplish. I don't want to try to be someone else, but I want You to work through me in my life, with what You have given me to do, to accomplish the things You want me to. Lead me, guide me, and show me how I can be the leader You desire. Show me how to be faithful to Your calling in my life. Change my heart so that my desires are Your desires. Help me to surrender to You more completely. Thank You for loving me, Lord."*

A FINAL WORD

We cannot discover all God has for us without seeking Him for it. That's the way God works. He draws us, we respond to Him and seek Him, and He begins to reveal those things to us that are in His heart for us. We have to be willing to obey His promptings to seek Him if we want to discover all He has for us. The good news, He wants to do this. He wants to reveal His will, His purpose, His love for us, and His direction for our life. He does it a step at a time. Are you ready to start taking steps with Him? He has a lot for you.

Being the leader God desires us to be is a part of being the person He wants us to be. His plan, His purposes for us, and our desire to follow Him are all involved in this. I encourage you to keep seeking and surrendering yourself to Him. Let Him take you on the adventure He has for you. Remember He has said, *"I will never leave you or forsake you"* (Hebrews 13:5).

ABOUT THE AUTHOR

Lou Turner wrote *Living Life God's Way* out of his passion for men to discover God, and to get to know Him and what He has for them. This 13-book men's discipleship series is the culmination of Lou's own journey—a life of seeking God, studying His Word, memorizing Scripture and meditating on it, and practical experience with family, community, marketplace work, and Christian ministry. It also comes, by Lou's own admission, from life experiences of both successes and mistakes, as a result of both good and bad decisions.

Lou has headed ministries, written and taught workshops, classes, and seminars, and discipled dozens of men. Now, he has put into print the things he has learned to help other men along their path and journey.

Most of Lou's growing up years were spent in Detroit and its suburbs, where he was raised in a pastor's home. Following his graduation from university with a Bachelor of Science in Business Administration, Lou and his wife planted and pastored a church for three years. After that time, he felt the strong call of God to return to business.

Over the years, Lou has served in numerous senior executive positions with national and international companies in the real estate and oil and gas industries. As of this writing, Lou is still active in business with his own home building company. He has been married to his wife Joan since they were 20. They have three children and 10 grandchildren and make their home in Phoenix, Arizona.

www.ingramcontent.com/pod-product-compliance
Lightning Source LLC
Chambersburg PA
CBHW021116080526
44587CB00010B/544